CW01507577

OUR HERITAGE

THE ROYAL LOGISTIC CORPS

TO COMMEMORATE
THE MILLENNIUM
AD·2000

OUR HERITAGE

THE ROYAL LOGISTIC CORPS

THE TRUSTEES OF THE REGIMENTAL ASSOCIATION TRUST
THE ROYAL LOGISTIC CORPS

Published in 2000 by the
Trustees of the Regimental Association Trust
The Royal Logistic Corps.

Copyright © The Trustees of the Regimental Association Trust
The Royal Logistic Corps.

All rights reserved. No part of this publication may be reproduced,
stored in a retrieval system, or transmitted in any form or by any means,
electronic, mechanical, photocopying, recording or otherwise
without the prior written permission from the copyright holder.

British Library Cataloguing-in Publication Data:
A catalogue record for this book is available from the British Library.

ISBN 0-9539011-0-6

Designed by Martin Richards
Edited by Judith Millidge
Produced by Roger Bonnett
World Print Limited, Hong Kong

FRONTISPIECE *The RLC Millennium Window in St Barbara's Church,
Deepcut, is dominated by the figure of the Risen Christ. Before Him are
grouped a young soldier in combat uniform, his wife and two children. Above
is the compass rose badge of the Worldwide Anglican Communion with its
motto in Greek, 'The truth shall make you free' (St John 8.32).*

*Three vignettes show Christian clergy sustaining soldiers across two
millennia. The window includes the rose, thistle, harp and dragon of the four
nations of the United Kingdom and a commemorative plaque. It was
dedicated on 31 October 1999 by the Revd. Dr V. Dobbin MBE QHC DD,
the Chaplain General.*

*The Millennium Window is the seventh window in St Barbara's Church
to have been commissioned from Goddard & Gibbs Studios Ltd and
designed by Mr J. N. Lawson FMGP. The earlier windows were donated by
the RAOC Training Centre, the RAOC in BAOR, the Surrey Branch of
the Normandy Veterans Association, the RAOC, the congregation of St
Barbara's Church and The RLC.*

CONTENTS

Her Royal Highness
The Princess Royal
Colonel-in-Chief

BUCKINGHAM PALACE

I am delighted to learn that The Royal Logistic Corps has decided to publish a book to remind those serving now and in the future of the Heritage that is the foundation of our Corps. History plays a vital role in linking the past with the present.

The Corps is only seven years old, but in that short time has shown itself to be key to effective operations all over the world and as a result has earned widespread praise for its achievements. The pride and purpose of our soldiers today is enhanced by their understanding that they are part of a long established tradition of supporting the Army in peace and war; this unique book will certainly give them a greater appreciation of those who have gone before them.

'Our Heritage' will serve to remind us all of the ethos and style of our predecessors. It is also a tribute to The Royal Logistic Corps and those who have been part of its history and I know it will inspire members of the Corps in the years to come.

His Royal Highness
The Duke of Gloucester
Deputy-Colonel-in-Chief

Her Royal Highness
The Duchess of Kent
Deputy-Colonel-in-Chief

Introduction

Director The Royal Logistic Corps

This fine book captures the heart and soul of the Corps of which I have the honour to be Director, and I am privileged to add my foreword. One of the first decisions I was called upon to make when I took over as Chairman of the Regimental Association Trustees in April 1999 was to confirm the Corps commitment to a variety of Millennium projects. I have a particular soft spot for the creation of 'Our Heritage', which, through its stunning photographs, brings to life the quite splendid paintings, silver, medals and museum artefacts belonging to The Royal Logistic Corps and inherited from our predecessors.

The production of 'Our Heritage', the second book published by The Royal Logistic Corps, has involved many already busy people in a lot of work to tight deadlines. My fellow Trustees and I are grateful to them all. This work shows that we are following in the footsteps, and maintaining the standards, of our predecessors. This is, of course, an ongoing process and it will be seen that we are not only very conscious and proud of our heritage but also committed to the continuing commissioning of works of art, both by painters and silversmiths. It is worth noting that regiments and messes of today also contribute to our heritage collection, in a way that did not happen in the past.

Our heritage is a matter for all of us, from the newest recruit to the most senior officer. We all contribute to the performance and efficiency of the Corps in our different ways. The publication of this book, linked with our extensive loan system which allows the whole Corps to use our treasures for special occasions, goes a long way to sharing our heritage at all levels. It has been a challenge, almost exhilarating, to put the book together. Hopefully our officers and soldiers will appreciate it for the Millennium masterpiece that it is.

ACKNOWLEDGEMENTS

The Trustees of the Regimental Association Trust, The Royal Logistic Corps established the Editorial Committee listed below. They were given overall responsibility for the production of the book as part of the Heritage Committee. The aim was to produce a fine publication for the Millennium that would tell the history of the Corps heritage through fine arts, medals and artefacts collected by The Royal Logistic Corps and Forming Corps.

Trustees

Brigadier T. Dalby-Welsh ADC
Chairman

Major-General D. L. Burden CB CBE

Major-General D. F. E. Botting CB CBE

Major-General M. S. White CB CBE DL

Brigadier T. McG. Brown OBE

Brigadier P. A. D. Evans OBE

Colonel K. M. Tutt OBE ADC

Colonel J. Astbury TD

Warrant Officer I (SSM) S. A. Yafai RLC

Warrant Officer I (RSM) C. Joinson RLC

Mr M. F. H. Adler TD

Lieutenant-Colonel J. G. Hambleton MBE – Regimental Secretary

Lieutenant-Colonel D. J. Owen MBE – Regimental Treasurer

Editorial Committee

Chairman: Colonel K. M. Tutt OBE ADC

Fine Arts: Lieutenant-Colonel J. G. Hambleton MBE

Medals: Lieutenant-Colonel D. J. Owen MBE

Advisor: Lieutenant-Colonel M. H. G. Young

Narrative: Dr A. R. Morton

Artefacts: Mr F. G. O'Connell

Particular members of the committee undertook the preparation of complete sections of the book, based on their specialised knowledge and expertise.

Sadly, during the production of this book Lieutenant-Colonel J. G. Hambleton MBE died. His friends on the Editorial Committee are grateful for his hard work, good humour and sound advice.

Most of the treasures and material photographed in the book, with the main exception of some silver and medals belonging to the Institution of the Royal Army Service Corps and Royal Corps of Transport, have been gifted to the Corps by our Forming Corps. Our grateful thanks go to the following for creating and preserving our heritage and making it available to The Royal Logistic Corps:

The Institution of the Royal Army Service Corps and Royal Corps of Transport

The Royal Army Ordnance Corps Charitable Trust

The Royal Pioneer Corps Association

The Army Catering Corps Association

Postal and Courier Service, Royal Engineers.

Photography by Alberto Gonzalez and Sergeant Penfold.

Sincere thanks go to Roger Bonnett who organised the production of the book and saw it safely through each stage. His advice was essential and of immense help. We are also deeply grateful to Lieutenant Colonel D. J. Owen MBE who coordinated the development of the book and the Regimental Headquarters staff for providing valuable administrative support.

Reproduction of *The Defence of Rorke's Drift* painting by Elizabeth Thompson, Lady Butler, is by kind permission of The Royal Collection © 2000 Her Majesty Queen Elizabeth II.

Inclusion in the book of the Cuneo paintings *Lull in the Battle 1984*, *Sword Beach D-Day* and *The Mouse Cartoon* is by kind permission of the Cuneo Fine Arts.

THE HISTORY AND COLLECTIONS OF
THE ROYAL LOGISTIC CORPS
AND ITS PREDECESSORS

THE HISTORY

Dr A. R. Morton

EARLY DAYS

The Royal Waggon Train in the Peninsular War, 1812 *(detail), painted by Johnny Jonas in 1993. The Royal Waggon Corps was raised in 1799, changing its name to the Royal Waggon Train in 1802. Having been formed in Bromley, Kent under the command of Lieutenant-Colonel Digby Hamilton (a friend of the Prince Regent), with five companies of 100 men each, the depot of the Royal Waggon Train moved to Croydon and expanded. In 1811 the uniform blue jackets were changed to red; a year later the Train adopted the new Light Dragoon shako, as depicted here. The Royal Waggon Train was awarded the battle honours Peninsula and Waterloo during the Napoleonic wars, but was disbanded in 1833 as a result of defence cuts, despite the objections of the Duke of Wellington.*

'The main and principal point in war is to secure plenty of provisions and to weaken or destroy the enemy by famine. An exact calculation must therefore be made before the commencement of the war as to the number of the troops and the expenses thereto, so that the provinces may in plenty of time furnish the forage, corn and all other kinds of provisions demanded of them to be transported.'

Flavius Vegetius, 4th century AD

In ancient times the Roman army was the only truly professional standing army in Europe, if not the world. Apart from the obvious technological differences, the Roman approach to war was very modern. As the quotation from the late fourth century AD Roman military author, Flavius Vegetius, demonstrates, the Romans were well aware of the importance of logistics. Roman field armies contained a well-organised baggage train with additional rations, spare tentage, replacement weapons and other equipment. Transport (waggons and pack animals) were assigned to individual legions and their sub-units (ten cohorts per legion, six centuries per cohort) and were driven by non-combatant 'servants'. Each legion was composed of approximately 5,000 professional soldiers whose weapons, equipment and white linen uniforms were supplied by the state.

Temporary supply bases were established behind the advancing army. In Britain following the successful invasion of AD 43, many of these supply bases later became permanent depots and eventually civilian settlements of some importance, such as Fishbourne and Chichester. During the Roman occupation of Britain the legions at different times built and garrisoned various permanent bases (fortresses), such as York, Caerleon, Usk and Wroxeter. Each base had workshops that produced weapons, pottery and other necessaries, granaries and medical facilities; the legion itself contained specialist soldiers, including quartermasters, storekeepers, butchers, engineers and priests. The vast network of good roads built by the legions in Britain and elsewhere in the empire allowed an efficient state postal and courier service to operate. The system depended on fast two-wheeled light chariots, with room for a driver and a dispatch carrier.

After a number of destructive civil wars in the late 4th century, the Roman garrison of Britain was finally withdrawn in AD 410 to assist in the defence of the empire's heartland, Italy. This did not prevent the final collapse of the Roman Empire in the west, but it did rob the province of Britannia of an efficient, disciplined, well-supplied and effective fighting force, many of whose personnel would have been recruited from native Britons by this time. It would take over a thousand years for the conduct of warfare in Britain, particularly in the field of military logistics, to approach the professionalism of the Roman military machine.

The various conflicts in Britain that occurred after the fall of Rome, first between invading Saxons and native Britons, later between the English kingdoms and Viking and Norman invaders, had much in common with the type of warfare practised in Britain before the arrival of the Romans. Armies were generally only formed for specific campaigns and consisted mainly of poorly armed foot soldiers with a small core of usually rich and well-equipped nobles. There was little uniformity in weapons and tactics were primitive, often consisting of two 'shield-walls' charging each other head on and depending on sheer staying power and attrition for victory.

Soldiers, most of whom were peasant farmers called away from their everyday agricultural tasks, provided their own weapons and equipment, the quality of which was almost entirely dependent on the personal finances of the warrior concerned. Only King Alfred the Great of Wessex (871–99), under constant pressure from Danish invaders, had the foresight to bring some order to military affairs. He began the construction of forts (known as 'burhs') to provide refuge for his people from Viking attacks and developed a complex system of military service, with landowners providing or paying for the defence of their nearest settlement. Nevertheless, although there is some evidence that early English armies relied on the class of free peasantry, known as 'ceorls' (churls), to bring some provisions to the battlefield, the supply system, such as it was, usually consisted of soldiers living off the land and devastating conquered territories, a practice which continued for centuries.

The great advantage of plunder was that it was a cheap method of supply. Most armies, however, became a disorganised rabble while looking for food and were highly vulnerable to attack. In most cases, there was no co-operation between the army and the local people. Another disadvantage was that campaigning usually had to be restricted to the summer, when food was readily available and the roads became usable for baggage trains. The most serious drawback, however, was the near impossibility of any form of long term logistic planning. There must have been many instances of armies running out of food before the successful conclusion of a campaign, as happened to a West Saxon force in 893. The Saxons, under the command of King Alfred's son, Edward, defeated a large Danish army at Farnham in Surrey and then pursued the survivors to an island on the River Colne north of Staines. Unfortunately, the ensuing siege came to a halt when the West Saxon force broke up and went home after their food ran out.

MEDIEVAL LOGISTICS 1066–1640

During the Middle Ages the feudal system imposed on England after the Norman Conquest of 1066 obliged nobles to supply a quota of soldiers to the Crown for the duration of a specific campaign, in exchange for land and titles. Although this made it relatively easy for a medieval monarch to raise an army, the feudal lords and barons ultimately sustained much of the cost. The knights of the crusades, for example, often found themselves bankrupt by the time they had provided arms for themselves and their servants. As unified nation states such as England and France came into being there was an increase in centralised government, which, together with a modest population increase, meant that larger armies could be raised at the outbreak of war. Soldiers did not yet wear a national uniform. The most competent soldiers were the retainers of individual nobles, who often wore the livery or badges of their respective lords. The generally poorly trained county levies wore their own civilian clothes.

Military developments during the Middle Ages included the building and destruction of heavily defended castles and other fortifications. Pioneers are first recorded as such in the records of the English garrison at Calais in 1346, at the beginning of the Hundred Years War with France. The pay and muster rolls show their rate of pay to have been between 4d and 6d a day, double or treble that of a foot archer, so their abilities were obviously highly valued. The advent of gunpowder during the 14th century brought a new dimension to military logistics. Cannon and smaller firearms required skilled manufacture and were beyond the pockets of the common soldier. Both their manufacture and management needed professional personnel, of a type that could not be raised by the feudal system of nobles supplying levies from their lands. In England this led to a reform of the feudal system known as the 'indenture' system. Feudal fees were now paid in coin to government tax collectors, enabling the Crown to hire specialist soldiers such as sappers, miners, engineers and gunners (artillerymen).

Records in the 14th century refer to the appointment to the royal household of an official known as the 'attilator' or 'artiller', the maker of cannon; from this title the word 'artillery' was derived. By the mid-15th century artillery and handguns were increasingly important. As the variety of arms and equipment grew, standards for their manufacture, known as 'ordinances', were laid down. In 1414 a Master of the Ordnance, one Nicholas Merbury, was appointed to obtain, store and issue all arms and warlike stores. The central arsenal and gunpowder store was established in the Tower of London, firmly under control of the Crown; later it became a government department known as the Board of Ordnance, under the direction of the Master of Ordnance. When the Yorkist King Edward IV invaded France in 1475 he employed William Rosse as Controller of the Ordnance, who was responsible for the king's guns, gunpowder, cannon balls, crossbows and bolts, bows and arrows, and arrow and bowstave timber (for replacement bows and arrows if needed). Rosse was also in charge of all English ships of 16 tons or over, as well as their crews.

Armies of the Middle Ages travelled slowly, their speed dictated by columns of waggons carrying tents, baggage and equipment. The earliest evidence for any sort of transport specialists in the English army comes from the Hundred Years War (1346–1453). At the battle of Agincourt in 1415, a 'Sergeant of the Waggons of the Household' served with the army of Henry V; in his campaign of 1422 the army also had a 'Master of the Baggage Train'. Henry's army had 25,000 horses and 'many carts and waggons', a huge organisation for the time. In 1461, some years after the end of the wars with France, Edward IV appointed one of his retainers, Richard Garnet, as 'Sergeant of the King's Pavilions'. Interestingly, Garnet was not only responsible for the tents of the royal household, but was also expected to fight with his 24 yeomen alongside the king.

Communications between a monarch and his or her armies were carried by the Royal Post, which as its name implies, was only for the use of the monarch and royal officials. Since the vast majority of people were illiterate, there was no need for a more wide-ranging postal service. In fact, it is significant that many of the logistic specialists that came into existence at this time are primarily concerned with the king's household, rather than with the needs of the common soldier.

Medieval army commanders were certainly aware of the importance of logistics in the prosecution of a war. *Knyghthode and Bataile,* a 15th century military manual, warned generals to 'Have purveyance of forage and victual for man and horse; for iron smiteth not so sore as hunger doth if food fail.' Nevertheless, although medieval soldiers were expected to provide and carry a small amount of rations themselves, and the army's baggage train carried extra stores (which soldiers had to pay for), much of their food and drink supplies still came from pillage. The larger the army, the more dev-astating the effect on the surrounding area. The situation was exacerbated during times of civil war, such as the Wars of the Roses (1455–85). In 1460 supply problems experienced by the northern Lancastrian army of Queen Margaret after their victory at the battle of Wakefield led to that army plundering its way south on a massive scale. This caused so much fear and panic across the land that much of the population of the south of England turned against her cause.

When Henry VIII came to the throne in 1509 he was determined to modernise the English army to enable him to pursue a vigorous foreign policy in Europe. At the beginning of his reign the army was still basically medieval in organisation, appearance, weapons and logistics. By the time of the king's death in 1547, however, the traditional longbow and 'brown bill' of the English infantryman were well on the way to being replaced by musket and pike. The rediscovery of classical learning that characterised the Renaissance extended to the art of war. Ancient military authors such as the Roman historian Vegetius were closely studied for ideas on how to improve contemporary military practice. In 1516 the position of 'Master of the Posts' had been established, whose function was to oversee the carriage of military dispatches and intelligence via a system of posting stages, horses and couriers. Later in the century, field armies raised for a campaign would be divided into regiments of ten companies each, based on the organisation of the ancient Roman legions.

Unfortunately, the supply and transport services did not attract the same attention as the rest of the army under King Henry. A large number of non-combatants followed Tudor armies, including pioneers, labourers, millers, bakers, etc., and, recorded for the first time in the campaign of 1544–46 against the French, female camp followers. Supplies were purchased from individual merchants, and although prices were fixed, the quality of provisions was variable. In 1545, for example, the English garrison of Boulogne was horrified to find that many barrels of meal and beef had become inedible because of careless packing. Transport problems also hindered the distribution of supplies. At least one campaign, that of 1523 against the French, ground to a halt because of the difficulties of obtaining the required number of waggons and waggoners to convey supplies from the supply dumps ('staples') to the army.

It was not until the reign of Queen Elizabeth I (1558–1603) that military logistics began to undergo serious modernisation. The wars of religion that erupted in Europe after the Reformation involved a number of English expeditionary forces which were sent to support French and Dutch Protestants. For the first time, the government shouldered the responsibility of feeding soldiers on active service, and in the later 16th century, the titles 'Proviant-Master-General' and 'Waggon-Master-General' first appeared. The Proviant-Master-General was responsible for 'providing victuals, corn, flesh, wine, bread and beer; for inspecting them; and issuing them to units according to their strengths'. He also stocked garrisons and fortifications with live edible beasts and birds. Answerable to the Treasury, he was provided with a lieutenant, a clerk, blacksmith, waggon-master, quartermaster and a number of 'directors'. The Waggon-Master-General oversaw the movement of baggage and stores. Answerable directly to the generals commanding the Horse and Foot, he was responsible for the waggon train, its order of march and its discipline.

The use of firearms by both infantry and cavalry increased throughout the 16th century and the Board of Ordnance extended its operations from the Tower of London to Woolwich and Rochester. The design of small arms and artillery improved constantly and the bore of cannon became more standardised. The Board's agents, the Commissaries of Ordnance, supplied all manner of 'warlike stores' with vital technical and scientific developments in small arms, artillery and ammunition emerging from the workshops and arsenal at Woolwich. Since warships were now armed with cannon, the Board of Ordnance also supplied arms and ammunition for the Royal Navy.

The Master of Ordnance, now known as the Master General of Ordnance, held an important political post as adviser to the monarch and Parliament on military matters. Later, great military men, such as the dukes of Marlborough and Wellington, would hold the post. Unfortunately, with the control of supplies under the Treasury, control of transport under the army and control of ordnance under Parliament, the efficiency of the army was inevitably to suffer from inter-departmental conflict and personal influence. This situation would not be better regulated until the end of the 19th century.

FROM THE CIVIL WAR TO THE 18TH CENTURY

'I had rather have a plain russet-coated captain that knows what he fights for, and loves what he knows, than which you call a gentleman and is nothing else.'

Oliver Cromwell

In England, the military experiences of the Civil War (1642–51) ultimately led to a departure from the old style of warfare. War broke out between King Charles I and his Parliament in England in 1642, and spread to Wales, Ireland and Scotland. In the first half of a war that lasted nine punishing years, both Royalist and Parliamentarian armies survived largely on requisition and acquisition, with no Commissariat magazines or transport available. Royalist documents relating to the battle of Edgehill in 1642, the first major conflict of the Civil War, show the king demanding 'Carts, Waynes and Horses' from the county of Shrewsbury 'upon payne of death'. Parliamentary documents for the same battle show that Parliament purchased 26 waggons from the civilian population for the use of civilian traders (known as sutlers), two waggons to be attached to each of the 13 regiments in the field army of the Earl of Essex. Both sides had supply problems: Royalist soldiers, whose pay was frequently in arrears, became particularly notorious for their poor treatment of local civilian populations as the war progressed.

Oliver Cromwell, an MP who raised his own well-disciplined cavalry regiment known as the 'Ironsides', soon rose to high command in the forces of Parliament. Rather than rely on mercenaries or poorly trained militia, Cromwell sought to place an efficient national army in the field. Together with Sir Thomas Fairfax, he created what became known as the New Model Army. The soldiers of the New Model Army were truly professional career soldiers: they were properly paid and not disbanded once the fighting was over. Soldiers were provided with standard equipment and basic rations. A 'Commissary-General of Victuals' was responsible for the daily issue of bread and cheese to every soldier. In contrast to the bewildering array of coat colours chosen at the whim of individual regimental colonels in both Royalist and earlier Parliamentarian armies, the infantry of the New Model Army were issued with a standard red coat, the first time that the state had issued a national uniform for the army. The red coat would be recognised the world over as the uniform of the British soldier for another 250 years.

The purchase and issue of supplies became the responsibility of civilians known as Commissaries. The Commissariat Department was formed in 1645 and eventually became part of the Treasury. The Commissariat were initially only financial agents providing money and negotiating contracts for the army, but during campaigns they bought stocks in anticipation of future needs and so became holders of stores. As Treasury agents, Commissariat officers were influential and independent, not always to the army's advantage.

Unlike its predecessors, the New Model Army had a headquarters organisation and the beginnings of a formal general staff, consisting of the Commissary-General of Victuals, a Commissary-General of Horse Provisions and a Waggon-Master General. Commissariat transport, much of it hired, carried rations, ammunition and the sick or wounded. The Artillery and Engineers had their own waggon trains under the Board of Ordnance, which itself was responsible for the procurement of artillery and other ordnance. Edward Prideaux was appointed by Cromwell to supervise communications between Parliament and its forces, but it seems that the army used and assisted the civilian postal service (set up in 1635) rather than establish its own organisation.

The standard of honesty in the administration of the New Model Army was exceptionally high and probably unique from an historical perspective. During the brief period of the Commonwealth, soldiering would become a respectable profession and attract officers and men of the highest quality and ability. The discipline of the New Model Army, inspired by religious idealism and enhanced by Cromwell's improvements in logistics, meant that there were very few incidents of abuse of unarmed civilians. This was a significant factor in the decision of many counties to switch their allegiance to Parliament as the war continued. After the victory of Parliament and the end of the Civil War in 1651 the New Model Army became the first professional standing army seen in Britain since the departure of the Roman legions over a thousand years before.

Military logistics in Britain continued to improve after the 'Glorious Revolution' of 1688, when the Dutch Prince William of Orange was invited by the English Parliament to become King William III of England, thus ensuring the Protestant succession. The first ration scale was authorised in 1689 and the post of Barrack-Master-General was established in 1699. The invention of the bayonet meant that there was no longer any need for pike-armed infantry to protect musketeers from cavalry attack. The flintlock musket had replaced the less efficient matchlock, thereby making the manu-

facture of flints an important industry. As an individual flint was only good for about 100 rounds, huge numbers were needed for the army. This need was met by the creation of a flint industry, which was based in the village of Brandon on the borders of Suffolk and Norfolk.

Further developments arose from the Duke of Marlborough's highly successful campaigns during the War of the Spanish Succession (1702–13). The war was fought to stop a French-backed candidate becoming king of Spain, and establishing France as the dominant power in Europe. Marlborough recognised the crucial importance of adequate rations and supplies, writing, 'No soldier can fight unless he is properly fed on beef and beer'. During his celebrated march to the Danube in 1704, which culminated in the battle of Blenheim, Marlborough stockpiled boots along his army's route. This ensured that his men always had good footwear and consequently were able to achieve a faster rate of march than their European counterparts.

Marlborough also developed a basic design for a military baggage waggon, a pattern which was to remain unchanged for many years, and which potentially meant that the army need no longer be faced with the problem of operating and maintaining civilian waggons of all shapes and sizes. He was determined to end the plunder system once and for all and ordered the Commissariat to provide fresh meat twice a week for his soldiers, although they had to pay for the privilege. These early efforts, however, continued to rely upon the presence of civilians. Civilians, who were not always reliable, still drove military transport waggons and civilian sutlers (male and female) were encouraged by the commissaries to follow regiments, providing fresh meat, vegetables and liquor, which soldiers could purchase to supplement their basic diet. A number of sutlers became extremely rich as a result, exploiting soldiers' natural desire for a more varied and interesting diet by charging exorbitant prices for their wares.

Many sutlers acquired a reputation (not always justified) for being shameless thieves. One exception, probably the most famous in Marlborough's army, was Mrs Christian Ross. In an effort to find her husband (serving in the Scots Greys) Mrs Ross concealed her sex and fought as a dragoon at the battles of Schellenberg (1704), Blenheim (1704) and Ramilles (1705), until she was wounded and her identity discovered in hospital. She was then reunited with her husband and continued to follow the British army as a sutler, gaining a reputation as a successful forager and a driver of a hard bargain, but also as one always ready to comfort a wounded or dying man. When she died in 1739 'Mother Ross' was buried in the Royal Hospital, Chelsea with full military honours.

Despite the shortcomings of relying on civilian drivers and sutlers, there is no doubt that Marlborough's attention to logistics contributed greatly to his army's ability to obtain a strategic advantage over the French time after time. As a result, French military power was broken after Marlborough's string of great victories in Bavaria and Flanders. Unfortunately, after the conclusion of the war in 1713, Marlborough's logistic organisation was closed down.

Throughout the 18th century, with the spread of Britain's influence overseas, soldiers were called upon to fight in India, Europe and the West Indies. The Board of Ordnance supplied the accommodation and fortifications needed to garrison outposts of Britain's growing empire. During the mid-18th century the Seven Years War (1756–63) resulted in the expulsion of France from North America and India. A number of amphibious operations were carried out by the British army, which required a greater degree of logistical planning and organisation than normal. Probably the most famous and significant of these was the capture of Quebec in 1759. Logistic support for the fleet and the 8,500-strong amphibious force tasked with the Canadian city's capture consisted of 102 transport ships, 13 ordnance vessels and four victualler's vessels.

In marked contrast to the often well planned and organised campaigns earlier in the century, very little thought was given to the army's logistic needs during the American War of Independence (1776–83). The war was fraught with the problems of insufficient troops and lack of supplies and transport. Inadequately prepared for the war, the British government was 3,000 miles, or a three-month sea journey, from the site of the conflict. Although the British army won the majority of land battles against the American colonists, serious logistic failure, exacerbated by the intervention of the combined fleets of France, Spain and Holland, led to disasters such as Saratoga in 1777, and ultimately Yorktown in 1781. The defeat at Yorktown at the hands of a Franco-American force led to American independence two years later.

At the end of the 18th century, the British government's alarm at the combination of revolution and imperial ambition in France saw the dispatch of military expeditions to the Netherlands, Egypt, Portugal and Spain. The growing sophistication of weapons, increasing size of armies and the global scale on which warfare now took place meant that armies were compelled to transport immense quantities of baggage and equipment far beyond the carrying capacity of the soldiers themselves. The need for a specialist military corps dedicated to supporting the army on campaign became increasingly obvious.

THE REVOLUTIONARY AND NAPOLEONIC WARS

It was not until the Duke of York raised an army to fight the forces of Revolutionary France in Flanders in 1794 that the need for an alternative system to operate military transport was finally recognised. The old system, reliant mainly on civilians, functioned slowly and often inefficiently, since each move during a campaign usually involved re-negotiating rates with dishonest or greedy locals, organising new drivers and coping with animals of varying strength, health and training. Following the recommendation of the Commissary-General serving with the Duke of York's army, the Corps of Waggoners was authorised by Royal Warrant on 7 March 1794. The Corps consisted of some 500 men under Captain James Pool, its main function being to provide transport services for the Commissariat.

It was hoped that greater efficiency and savings could be achieved if soldiers were recruited, trained and equipped specifically as a transport organisation, to supplement the huge variety of hired civilian waggons and pack animals. With poor quality soldiers (many of the Corps of Waggoners personnel were released prisoners, which earned the unit the nickname 'Newgate Blues') and no effective leadership, the transport organisation fared badly, but no worse than others on the campaign. On their return to England in 1796 the Waggoners were disbanded, but the Corps was at least the first wholly military unit devoted to logistics.

Another transport organisation, the Royal Waggon Corps, was established in 1799 for an expedition to the Low Countries under the command of Sir Ralph Abercrombie. In 1802 its name was changed to the Royal Waggon Train. Although small, the Royal Waggon Train did sterling work in Spain, supporting Wellington's army in his campaign against Napoleon's marshals. They were able to provide a specialist transport service to complement the bulk of locally hired transport still used by the Commissariat, which at this time still controlled the majority of army transport, with some 400 bullock carts and 12,000 pack animals. Conditions in Spain tested the organisation of the Royal Waggon Train to the full; they had to cover huge distances, sometimes in appalling weather conditions, and negotiate with unreliable sources and often uncooperative Spaniards. As a result of the Royal Waggon Train's achievements, it was awarded the battle honour Peninsula. Wellington's campaigns in Spain and north-west Europe culminated in the final defeat of Napoleon at Waterloo, which ended French dreams of dominating Europe. The Royal Waggon Train was subsequently awarded the battle honour Waterloo for its contribution to Wellington's victory.

At about the same time as the creation of the Corps of Waggoners, the Ordnance Field Train was raised. The Field Train was responsible for the conveyance and issue of ordnance in the field, and its personnel also supervised the movement of guns. Although the Ordnance Field Train was under the control of the civilian Board of Ordnance, an artillery officer was appointed Director-General of the Field Train to introduce a military element into its administration. At the beginning of a campaign the Field Train would establish a depot

The field of Waterloo as it appeared the morning after the memorable battle of the 18th June 1815. *A painting by John Heaviside Clark. The Royal Waggon Train is depicted in its post-battle role of removing the dead and wounded from the battlefield, a gruesome task that took 12 days. It was at this decisive battle that Private Brewster of the Royal Waggon Train distinguished himself. The British and German garrison of Hougoumont Château, an important strongpoint in Wellington's line, had been repeatedly attacked by French troops throughout the day. The defending troops had expended most of their ammunition and would have undoubtedly had to surrender the building if Private Brewster had not managed to drive an ammunition waggon through the French lines to resupply the garrison. After the battle Private Brewster was awarded a medal normally reserved for officers and promoted. He later transferred to the Guards.*

at the base of operations, and forward depots as required. During the Waterloo campaign of 1815 the base depot was at Antwerp, with advanced depots at Brussels and Vilmorden. The contribution of the Board of Ordnance to the final victory over Napoleonic France was not restricted to land warfare. The efficiency of the percussion locks fitted to British naval cannon gave the Royal Navy a decided advantage over the Franco-Spanish fleet defeated at Trafalgar in 1805.

Communication between the seat of government and an army in the field is an essential for co-ordinated military success and in this matter the army in Spain was well served, in spite of the distances involved. A weekly ship from Falmouth to Lisbon delivered official mail as well as private correspondence, of which there was relatively little, since most soldiers still could not read or write. Private mail passed to the Quartermaster-General, who had two Sergeant Postmasters, but the service was difficult and unreliable; an additional problem was the reluctance of many recipients to pay the postage costs.

After Waterloo the steady development of logistics was halted. The nation, tired of years of conflict, soon dismantled the army's support services. The Ordnance Field Train was disbanded as soon as the Napoleonic wars were over. The Royal Waggon Train was disbanded in 1833, as part of a major reduction in the size of the army. A famous song of the time summed up society's attitude to its soldiers succinctly:

'In time of war, when dangers near they gave us beef and beer. Now Boney's beat, we've naught to eat,and they have naught to fear.'

THE CRIMEAN WAR AND AFTER

In 1854 British and French troops were sent to the Crimea to support Turkey, in an effort to curtail Russian imperialism. The drastic defence cuts imposed after Waterloo meant that at the outbreak of the Crimean War the British army had no permanent military logistic organisation. Each soldier arrived in the Crimea with one blanket, three days pork and biscuit, but no tentage; there was no regimental transport, no supply system and bad weather caused unimaginable hardship. A much-reduced Commissariat was expected to support a force of 33,000 men with only 75 mules and a few carts, with instructions from the Treasury to operate as cheaply as possible.

The few Commissaries present, under the command of the Peninsular War veteran Commissary-General Filder, found it impossible to cope with the demands of an army that had landed with inadequate supplies. No one had any idea of the type and quantity of provisions required. No thought had been given to the clothing and housing of soldiers in a rigorous climate. Units were left to demand supplies almost at a whim, often competing for limited resources. The lack of fresh rations and hygienic facilities was of particular concern. To make it worse, an epidemic of cholera spread throughout the army and animals starved through shortage of fodder. Because of a lack of communication between the different agencies involved, the army's administration was a disaster and, despite

'Commissariat Difficulties', from a collection of Crimean War sketches by William Simpson, 1855, entitled The Seat of War in the East. *The scene depicts the problems of a supply convoy at Kadikoi, during wet weather on the unsurfaced road from Balaclava to Sebastopol. The sketch is accompanied by a poem: addressed to the 'Shade of Tarmacadam', it bemoans the lack of surfaced roads in the Crimea and looks forward to the inauguration of the railway line from Balaclava to Sebastopol. Built by civilian engineers, it was the first railway used to support the army.*

Herculean efforts on the part of individuals, health and morale were at a low ebb.

As a result of the exposure of logistic inadequacies in the Crimea, two new corps were formed: a Hospital Conveyance Corps for the sick and wounded, and an Army Works Corps. The Commissariat was transferred from the Treasury to the Horse Guards, and in January 1855 a Land Transport Corps was established under its Director-General, Colonel W. M. S. McMurdo. The new Land Transport Corps was charged 'with the land transport of all stores, supplies and necessaries at all times required by our army in the field'. Raised largely in London, the Corps was classed as cavalry and divided into two wings, each intended to alternate as echelons on different days. Each wing comprised six divisions, one for each division of the Expeditionary Force, totalling 48 officers, 2,270 British soldiers, 5,800 natives and a carrying capacity of 19,200 mule loads. This organisation soon changed, but for the first time supply was allocated to individual fighting formations, removing both the need and opportunity for units to 'steal' supplies intended for others.

One of the consequences of the disastrous failure of the logistics arrangements during the Crimean War was the disbandment of the Board of Ordnance in 1855. A serious problem that had been faced by the Commissaries of Ordnance in particular was that, as civilians and specialists, they were not considered part of the army. They were excluded from the army's overall planning and thus could not judge if the ordnance stores and other materiel requested by individual units were related to their actual needs. In addition, army officers, most of whom acquired their commissions because of their wealth and social connections rather than on merit, were not experienced or knowledgeable enough to know what to ask for. The Board's responsi-

bility to provide 'warlike stores' for the army was passed between a variety of corps and departments that evolved, amalgamated and disbanded throughout the latter half of the 19th century until the formation of a permanent military organisation, the Army Ordnance Corps, in 1896.

The suffering of British soldiers in the Crimea was brought to the attention of the British public by one of the first newspaper war correspondents, William Russell of *The Times*. His reports, carried under an early arrangement between Britain and France for the carriage of mail to the troops, sparked a flurry of activity on the part of Lord Aberdeen's government, which later fell from office as a result of the public outcry. Florence Nightingale and the French chef Alexis Soyer were dispatched to investigate and improve the troops' medical treatment, as well as their living conditions and culinary support.

Florence Nightingale, although better known for her hospital work, was also a superb organiser and administrator. In the face of appalling bureaucracy — on one occasion a consignment of badly needed shirts could not be opened until a Board of Officers had been convened a fortnight later — she managed to get a special combined supply depot opened at Scutari. Ignoring official regulations, she was able to effect a prompt distribution of military equipment, food and medical supplies to where they were most needed.

Soyer, a well-known Victorian chef-de-cuisine, developed a variety of simple recipes and cooking techniques and introduced the Soyer Stove, the basis of many a welcome brew in subsequent campaigns. He also introduced soldiers to basic concepts of hygiene such as boiling water before drinking it. In fact the Crimean War was the first occasion when the army started to look seriously at catering. Food in individual regiments was still prepared by those who were 'blessed with some culinary talent or who were failing in any other skill', and the introduction of the Soyer stove initiated a mobile form of cooker to provide hot food for the soldier from a central, regimental source. This was followed by the development of training camps at home, and of the 'Aldershot Oven', which saw service into the Second World War.

Sergeant Cooks were authorised in all regiments of the army in 1870; and in 1883 the first Instructional Kitchen was opened in Salamanca Barracks, Aldershot. It may have been only a small school to train Messing Officers, but there had been no formal cookery training in the army before that. Command Cookery Schools were the next development and were established by the Army Service Corps before the First World War, becoming responsible for cookery training in the army until 1941.

In common with the rest of society, the level of literacy in the British army continued to rise during the 19th century. A greater number of soldiers were both willing and able to write letters home, and the need for a postal service dedicated entirely to the needs of the army became increasingly obvious. In the Crimea mail was still a civilian responsibility, however, although clerks were obtained from the military to help with sorting mail and identifying the position of units. At first, the French post office system conveyed post destined for British forces; later, ships of the Royal Navy were used, but this proved even more unreliable. Some two million letters passed between Britain and the Crimea and the postal organisation was hard-pressed; obtaining payment from the recipient often created problems. The Crimean War would prove to be the last occasion when civilian postal staff were sent into the field with the British army.

THE INDIAN MUTINY AND COLONIAL WARS 1857–99

The difficulties experienced in the Crimea firmly underlined the need for permanent military logistic services. Nevertheless, confusion persisted throughout the campaigns in China (1860), India (1857–58, 1863), Abyssinia (1867) and the myriad small-scale conflicts in Africa (1887-1895). Disagreements between the huge variety of short-lived military support units and the Commissaries reflected conflict between the military authorities and the Treasury in London.

In 1856 the Land Transport Corps was replaced by the seven-battalion Military Train, with each battalion designed to support one of the army's seven divisions. The Train was fully combatant and ranked in the Army Lists after the most junior cavalry regiment. Since

many of its soldiers had transferred from cavalry regiments, they were only too happy not to be employed in transport and supply roles in the two overseas campaigns for which the Military Train is well-known, the Indian Mutiny and the New Zealand Maori Wars.

On the outbreak of the Indian Mutiny (1857–58) the 2nd Battalion Military Train was diverted while en route to China to India, where it was equipped as light cavalry. It was at Nathapur, during the battle of Azimghur, Lucknow in April 1858 that Farrier Michael Murphy and Private Samuel Morley were awarded the Victoria Cross for saving the life of Lieutenant Hamilton, Adjutant of the 3rd Sikh Cavalry. When the battalion left Calcutta at the end of its tour, a special congratulatory order was issued and a salute of guns fired. The Military Train earned the battle honours 'Lucknow' and, from subsequent service in China, 'Taku Forts' and 'Pekin'.

In 1864 during the wars with the Maoris in New Zealand (1861–71), the 4th Battalion Military Train was deployed to Auckland. A Commissariat Corps had already been formed in the colony for the purposes of logistic support; and as the Military Train was ordered to restrict its operations to the area around Auckland, there was little opportunity to distinguish itself. As a result the Military Train's one moment of glory was a cavalry charge against the Maoris at Nukmaru, during which the 4th Battalion's Captain Witchell received a commendation for leading a successful charge over difficult ground.

The efforts of the military authorities to wrest control of the logistic role from the hands of civilians had reached a turning point with the disbandment of the Board of Ordnance in 1855. The days of the civilian Commissaries of the Commissariat were also numbered. Subsequent years saw the formation, amalgamation and disbandment of a bewildering variety of units and departments. The period from the end of the 1860s is complicated and any full account would be unreadable. In outline, however, a wholly military Control Department was formed in 1869, which was basically an officer corps designed to control a supply and transport sub-department. The latter consisted primarily of the Army Service Corps, whose personnel included volunteers from the now defunct Military Train, and the Military Stores Staff Corps that had been formed in 1865 by Royal Warrant. On formation the Army Service Corps consisted of 12 transport companies and ten supply companies, with No 1 (Depot) Company based at Aldershot.

In 1876 the Control Department was split up and replaced by a Commissariat and Transport Department and Ordnance Store Department, all under a Surveyor-General of Ordnance in the War Office. In 1877 the Ordnance Store Companies of the Army Service Corps were separated from the supply and transport units and concentrated at Woolwich under the Ordnance Store Branch of the Army Service Corps.

Following the Crimean War, close links between the army and the post office had been formed. After unfruitful recommendations to convert the 49th Middlesex Rifle Volunteers to a postal corps in 1877, a Royal Warrant dated 22 July 1882 authorised the formation of the Post Office Corps, and the 24th Battalion Middlesex Volunteers were allocated for this service in the Egyptian and Sudanese campaigns. Four Senior NCOs, four corporals and 35 men embarked for Egypt, making a promising start under difficult circumstances. The first link was made with the Royal Engineers during the Sudan campaign to save General Gordon in Khartoum, as the Engineers controlled the telegraphy service used by the Post Office Corps in the course of their duties.

Of the many small colonial wars fought by the British army during the second half of the 19th century, the Zulu War of 1879 is undoubtedly one of the most famous. One Assistant-Commissary, James Langley Dalton, was awarded the Victoria Cross for his outstanding bravery at Rorke's Drift on 22 January 1879, when 4,000 Zulu warriors launched numerous assaults on the mission station-turned-supply depot. Unfortunately, the logistic services as a whole were not able to cope with the demands made on them during the Zulu War. There was a general shortage of waggons and political and economic factors made it difficult to hire or commandeer local transport. Also, the three

Army Service Corps companies sent as reinforcements from England were equipped with General Service (GS) Waggons designed for use in Europe, and could not cope with the rough South African veldt.

In January 1880, as a result of its perceived failures, the Commissariat and Transport Department was redesignated the Commissariat and Transport Staff. Officers of this corps commanded Army Service Corps companies until August 1881 when the Army Service Corps, another casualty of the Zulu War, was abolished and replaced by the Commissariat and Transport Corps. There were two main depots where its personnel were trained: Aldershot for Horse Transport and Supply, and Woolwich for Horse Transport. The most important result of the abolition of the Army Service Corps at this time was that its Ordnance Store Companies were no longer part of a transport and supply corps but were instead absorbed into a new Ordnance Store Corps, later to become part of the Royal Army Ordnance Corps.

General Sir Redvers Buller VC became Quartermaster-General in 1887 and used his experience in Africa and Canada and advice from the last of the Commissary-Generals, Sir Edward Morris, to create a second Army Service Corps in 1888. He insisted that, for the first time since the Peninsular War, transport and supply units should be staffed by combatant officers of high calibre, wearing the same uniform and badges as their men. As an early sign of changing times the first logistic officer to go to the Staff College was Major R. H. L. Warner ASC in 1894.

Meanwhile, the Quartermaster-General's office in Whitehall was less interested in the world of Ordnance, since stores and munitions were not perceived as an everyday requirement in peacetime, and unnecessary holdings were expensive. Ordnance officers did not

A montage from the end of the 19th century showing the second Army Service Corps (formed in 1888) at work and the uniforms of its predecessors, artist unknown. The centrepiece shows an attack by Zulus on a supply convoy during the war of 1879. Around the centrepiece are (clockwise from top left) scenes depicting a shoeing smith, an ambulance waggon, butchers, bakers, a forage depot, pack animals on the march in Egypt and a supply convoy at the halt. Beneath are the uniforms of the Royal Waggon Train (1800, 1820), the Military Train (1856, 1870), the officer-only Control Department (1874) and the 'present day' Army Service Corps.

hold combatant commissions and were not eligible for staff appointments; their technical skills, considerably in excess of other regimental officers, were smothered and frustrated in the army inefficiency of the day. In 1896, however, reforms were adopted which imposed a form of rationalisation in storekeeping and accounting, improved training, pay and ordnance matters, as well as amalgamating five branches into an Army Ordnance Department and Corps. These branches were the Ordnance Store Department and four Inspectorates (General Stores, Warlike Stores, Small Arms and Guns).

This reorganisation was largely the work of a brilliant administrator, Colonel John Steevens, who was later to become the first Colonel-Commandant of the Royal Army Ordnance Corps. Collar badges incorporating elements of the coat of arms of the old Board of Ordnance were also taken into use in 1896.

Finally, at the beginning of the 20th century, all logistic support for the British Army was in the hands of serving soldiers, in the form of the Army Service Corps, the Army Ordnance Corps and the Army Post Office Corps.

SOUTH AFRICA 1899-1902

'War in South Africa would be one of the most serious wars that could possibly be waged.'

Joseph Chamberlain

The Boers were the descendants of Dutch settlers who undertook a great trek north from South Africa's Cape Colony in the 1830s to escape British rule, in particular to avoid the effects of the abolition of slavery throughout the British empire. Independent republics had subsequently been established by the Boers among the numerous and often mobile local tribal groups of southern Africa. These republics were seen by many as brutally racist towards black Africans, even in a period much less liberal than today. The presence of British colonists in the area reassured the British government, who were concerned about the security of the sea route to India. For nearly a century these three groups maintained an uneasy but stable co-existence, but the discovery of diamonds and gold destroyed this fragile peace. Paul Kruger, President of the Transvaal, enacted harsh measures in his republic

against the mainly British immigrants, who were denied the right to vote and subjected to much higher taxation than Boer citizens. Many Boers were also afraid that Britain was going to enfranchise all black Africans throughout South Africa.

British attempts to establish a controlling interest, first by negotiation and subsequently by force (the Transvaal War or first Boer War of 1880–81), met with disaster when a British force was defeated by the Boers at Majuba Hill. At Isandhlwana in 1879 the Zulus had demonstrated that British troops could be beaten. The Zulus were subsequently defeated in the war of 1879, but the blow to British prestige had been tremendous. At Majuba Hill in 1881 the Boers had dealt another blow to British military prowess. Although the power of the Zulus and other tribal groups had been subdued by the British, to the advantage of Boer settlers, the ill-defined peace between the Boers and the British colonists after 1881 was even more strained, and the atmosphere filled with resentment.

In 1899 the inevitable conflict broke out when the

Boers invaded Cape Colony and Natal and besieged the towns of Kimberley, Ladysmith and Mafeking. The invaders proved themselves quite willing to fire artillery shells into besieged towns packed with women and children. The British expectation of a short war was shattered and fighting lasted for three years. The government found itself committed to a vast expenditure and became increasingly pressurised by the public. With the development of an efficient postal service, letters from the front and newspaper reports brought the events in South Africa to the population at home at a speed never before experienced, which greatly helped influence public opinion.

After the experience gained in the Red River Expedition in Canada (1869–70), the Ashanti War (1873–74), the South African Wars of 1879–81, Egypt and the Sudan (1882–85) and a host of other campaigns in Africa, the Army Service Corps was experienced and well-organised. Unfortunately, the South African War of 1899–1902 posed logistical problems of which the contemporary British army had no experience — the lessons of the Peninsular War were long forgotten.

The Braemar Castle. *A painting by W. Parkyn. At the outbreak of the Boer War in 1899 the Army Service Corps had only been in existence for 11 years. The war in South Africa would prove to be the greatest challenge yet to the newly formed corps. On 6 October 1899 the troopship sailed from England for South Africa with almost the entire Army Service Corps (over 3,000 men) on board. Today, it is inconceivable that the entire logistic support element of an expeditionary force would be transported in one ship. The Braemar Castle was later sunk during the First World War while trooping in the Aegean in 1916.*

The area of operations was vast and the means of communication poor. The total strength of the forces employed against the Boers, including colonial and irregular troops, peaked at 450,000 men. Virtually the entire Army Service Corps — over 3,000 men — were sent to South Africa.

The Army Service Corps formed the main transport links forward of the railheads, with companies split into two parts, and operated depots on the lines of communication for food, forage and ammunition. In the first year of the war British forces suffered a number of bloody defeats at Stormberg, Magersfontein and, worst of all, Colenso. It was at the battle of Colenso, on 15 December 1899, that the Army Service Corps achieved distinction. Early in the war some 600 ASC Drivers had been attached to the Royal Artillery to replace their casualties. At Colenso a body of artillerymen and drivers managed to recover two guns under heavy Boer fire. For this and other actions the Army Service Corps later received a commendation from the Commander-in-Chief, Lord Roberts. For its part in the war as a whole the Army Service Corps was honoured in 1902 with the appointment of Queen Victoria's son, HRH The Duke of Connaught, as its Colonel (later Colonel-in-Chief).

Over 1,000 soldiers and NCOs of the Army Ordnance Corps, led by officers of the Army Ordnance Department, were deployed to South Africa. With little experience in the field, the Army Ordnance Corps improvised a supply for ordnance stores as the campaign developed, and bravely surmounted its most pressing difficulties. Among the many responsibilities of the corps were contracting for and issuing the vast quantities of khaki uniform which now replaced the red coat as the standard uniform of the British soldier. The corps manned a 23-acre depot in Bloemfontein

housed entirely in tents, which was established to meet the requirements of the artillery. The field guns already present in the Cape at the beginning of the war were in such bad condition that they needed complete refurbishment, as did their ammunition. Both the Army Ordnance Corps and the Army Ordnance Department were designated as non-combatant and were still regarded as specialists and outsiders by the rest of the army. As in the Crimea, Ordnance soldiers and their officers were frequently excluded from the planning and decision-making process, and as a result they were unable to bring their expertise to bear on plans for future campaigns.

A Post Office Corps had been formed in 1877, followed by a second Army Postal Corps called the Royal Engineers Telegraph Reserve — both were reorganised into two supplementary companies. In October 1899 63 men left for South Africa, with others to follow. The HQ and Base Post Office were established in Cape Town and field post offices were set up in the Cape and Natal. Difficulties soon abounded: Captain Treble, the Army Postmaster, did not receive the assistance he needed from either the Post Office or the War Office in the early months of the war, and information on unit locations was hard to come by. For the first time the mobility of units, both British and Boer, presented great difficulties to those trying to maintain a link with home, although determination and dedication, as well as the assistance of 100 reinforcements in 1900, ensured their eventual success.

As well as problems of transport there was of course the matter of security; like their comrades in the rest of the army, Post Office Corps personnel risked attack from Boer commandos. One of many such incidents occurred on 7 June 1900, when Lieutenant P. J. Preece and 18 men of the Army Post Office Corps were part of a 160-strong force at Roodewal railway station, guarding 2,000 bags of mail, winter clothing for 20,000 men and other stores needed by Lord Roberts' army. The station came under attack from 1,200 Boers and five artillery pieces under the command of General Christian De Wet. After offering stiff resistance, the out-numbered defenders were forced to surrender. The survivors, including Lieutenant Preece, became prisoners of war.

Nevertheless, the Army Post Office Corps expanded and rapidly gained experience. By the end of the war 630 officers and men had taken part, and 500,000 letters and newspapers as well as 12,000 parcels had been delivered to the troops each week. With the increase in the use of and the improvements in the railway, the war also saw the introduction of Travelling Post Offices.

Once British commanders had come to terms with the efficiency, mobility and armament of the Boers, their tactics changed and the major Boer cities were easily captured. The Boers, however, continued to fight a mobile guerrilla war, which the British could only counter by burning farms, clearing the veldt and gathering Boer families into special camps. The public greeted the initial victories with parades and celebration, but as news filtered through of the soldiers' conditions and the death rates in internment camps, the celebrations turned to protest. For the first time the public felt a close involvement with a foreign war. Peace was negotiated in 1902 after the Boer commandos were finally defeated by General Lord Kitchener. Ultimately, the Boer republics became part of the Union of South Africa, the original aim of British policy in that region.

In the aftermath of the Boer War, like that of the Zulu War 20 years before, the wartime performance of the logistic services came under close scrutiny. The Army Service Corps and Army Ordnance Department had been put in place early in the campaign but not in adequate numbers. The officers and men worked day and night, adapting well to local conditions. Their efforts, however, were frequently thwarted by a stream of ignorant, confusing and contradictory orders issued from higher military authorities. In consequence, the troops often went hungry and animals frequently starved. Ironically, the earlier civilian organisations, the Commissariat and the Board of Ordnance, had to a certain extent been able to operate independently of army commanders who, with some exceptions, had not built up any experience or understanding of how to use a logistic organisation. As a result of these experiences, Lord Esher headed a committee in 1904 which reorganised the command structure of the army and created a General Staff, which sadly contained no logistic corps officers for some time.

One important consequence of the fighting in South African War was that the Army Service Corps was given responsibility for all mechanical transport in the army in 1902. There was initially some resistance to mechanisation from various quarters in the army. An incident during the war when a traction engine had managed to recover a bogged-down waggon, which 80 oxen had failed to move, made many aware of the potential benefits to logistic operations of the new technology. The Army Service Corps took over a handful of steam engines from the Royal Engineers who had used them in South Africa, as well as a few cars.

The principle was also established that the operator would repair his own equipment, the first mechanical transport (MT) workshop being established in

Aldershot in 1905. Automobiles were purchased for use as staff cars from 1902 onwards and the first mechanical transport unit, 77 Company ASC, was formed in Aldershot in 1903. With steam and combustion engines developing at a pace, a number of mechanical transport companies soon came into being, but the horse still remained the main means of locomotion for the army until after the First World War.

After the Boer War, Field Post Offices were used increasingly on manoeuvres and it was agreed that the Army Postal Corps should continue as a reservist organisation; but this decision somehow got lost in the reorganisation of the Volunteer Army. In 1908, however, the new establishment of the Territorial Army contained provision for postal detachments in all 14 divisions. After several years, the link with the Royal Engineers (as the Postal Section) was formalised in 1913.

THE FIRST WORLD WAR 1914–18

In the early years of the 20th century many people in Europe anticipated a 'Great War', a term which was in use well before war broke out. Kaiser Wilhelm's ambition to build a huge German empire aroused fears throughout Europe, where the various nations had established a complex network of alliances which, with a spark in Serbia, drew the whole continent into war. The initial German plan relied heavily on a rapid movement through Belgium to attack France. This invoked a defensive agreement between Britain and Belgium, however, and saw the beginning of the long static conflict in Belgium and northern France.

After the declaration of war in August 1914, the Army Service Corps and Ordnance Services were to expand enormously. With the reforms which followed the South African War and the widespread indications that war was imminent, the logistic services were well prepared to project an army into Europe. Effective plans had been laid to mobilise men and resources and, although the conflict soon devoured all that could be provided, the basic organisation, combined with hard work, meant that the demands made by the British army on its logistic services could just about be met.

Transport and the provision of food, water, fuel and fodder were the responsibilities of the Army Service Corps. With a combination of animal transport and the new steam and petrol technology, the Army Service Corps transported their own supplies, as well as personnel and materiel supplied by the Ordnance. During the war Army Service Corps responsibilities expanded greatly to include the provision of fuel, fuel tankers, vehicles and drivers for all HQs, medical units and non-Army Service Corps units, the Expeditionary Force Canteen and motor cycle orderlies; all heavy guns of the Artillery were towed, Engineer pontoon parks transported and even Signal Section mobile pigeon lofts driven. As the war progressed 83,000 men were transferred to the Infantry to replace casualties or in exchange for men of a lower medical category because of serious manpower shortages in the BEF and over 100 officers were transferred to the Royal Flying Corps. The rations supplied by the Army Service Corps were a distinct improvement on those available in previous conflicts, but the preparation of food was still in the hands of amateurs.

Army Service Corps personnel were also involved

London Omnibus on the Western Front. *A painting by F. Matania. In August 1914 60 AEC 'B' type omnibuses in their original livery and with their civilian drivers were requisitioned by the Admiralty to transport a force of Royal Marines to Antwerp to counter the German attack in Belgium. A few months later, 300 more omnibuses were taken over by the army for the first battle of Ypres (October-November 1914), this time driven by ASC drivers. Painted battleship grey, each bus could carry 25 fully armed men.*

in the development and employment of the British secret weapon designed to break the stalemate of trench warfare — the tank. In 1915 711 Company ASC was chosen as the MT workshop for the newly created Heavy Branch of the Machine Gun Corps, later known as the Tank Corps when secrecy was no longer necessary. Although volunteers to crew the tanks came from every regiment and corps of the British army, the drivers were always from the Army Service Corps. About 50 tanks were used at the battle of Flers-Courcelette on 15 September 1916. After this first battle involving tanks, most of the ASC drivers transferred directly into the Tank Corps and later took part in the largest tank engagement of the war, at Cambrai in 1917.

The huge task of supplying ammunition and weapons fell to the Army Ordnance Corps. They also maintained the weapons and supplied all of the soldiers' clothing and equipment. A Base Ordnance Depot was set up at Le Havre, with subsidiary depots at Rouen and Boulogne, and large ammunition dumps were established in the forward areas to ease the problem of resupply. Similarly, the Army Service Corps had depots at Le Havre, Calais, Rouen and Abbeville. The routine system of supply was from the UK base, through a variety of ports to the continent, then from base depots to advanced depots; rail movement was used from the base to the depots on the continent, thence to a railhead. Divisional horse transport collected from railheads for distribution to forward units, with third line mechanical transport being responsible for the delivery of ammunition to the heavy artillery.

The long period of static warfare in France and Belgium led to the expenditure of ammunition on an unprecedented scale. Mass production resulted in a heavy burden on the Army Ordnance Corps in the field of supply and storage; the inspection, repair of ammunition and other technical ammunition work were undertaken on a scale never attempted outside Woolwich Arsenal. Schools were established to train officers and NCOs to deal not only with the new types of ammunition produced during the war, but also with German ammunition. Whereas the Army Service Corps was responsible for vehicle workshops, the Army Ordnance Corps operated workshops for artillery, including mobile workshops well forward. Wear and tear on the guns placed a tremendous strain on the technical staff who had to keep the weapons in action. For the first time, too, Ordnance was represented in each division, with a Deputy-Assistant Director Ordnance Services (a major) and a staff sergeant-major being responsible for all ordnance services. They were later given sufficient staff to deal with the flow of stores in divisional HQ and within the division. All this allowed for a better co-ordination of logistic support in the field.

Another major problem that arose from the immense size of the army supported on the continent, was labour. In August 1914 the Army Service Corps established labour companies to handle the huge volume of supplies flowing through ports and into Europe. Consisting of some 530 men each, the companies carried out manual tasks at depots and ports as well as on the lines of communication. They worked alongside other units of non-combatant and prisoner-of-war labour, all of which would later be incorporated into the Labour Corps. The Royal Engineers and Ordnance Depots, too, soon required large amounts of labour and in 1915 calls were made on South Africa, the West Indies, China and India to supply personnel. By 1916 42,000 men were employed. In January 1917 all of these were combined with Pioneer battalions of infantry regiments to form a new Labour Corps. At the end of the war, over 300,000 men were serving in the Labour Corps. Having made a considerable contribution to the war effort, the Labour Corps was disbanded in 1919 and it was not until 1939 that its vital contribution to military logistics was recognised once again.

On the outbreak of war, 300 men of the Postal Section left immediately with the British Expeditionary Force for France, leaving only 30 men in England. The Postal Home Depot remained in London (originally at Mount Pleasant) but the enormous increase in mail caused it to be moved several times, including to Regent's Park. In 1917, part of the work was diverted to main post offices in cities such as Manchester, Leeds, Sheffield, Bristol, Birmingham and Glasgow. Mails for the continent were moved initially via Southampton to Le Havre, and later via Folkestone to Boulogne. As in previous wars, security was a major problem, and unit location information was scarce. Some of those in command believed that that mail was a luxury and should have no priority over supply ships, trains or transport columns. The use of railheads and refilling points for mail was risky because of the changing tactical situation, so it was not long before independent transport means were used and it was normal for mail to arrive in a forward trench just two days after being posted in the UK.

Throughout the war postal staff had to battle constantly against a lack of shipping space, unsympathetic planners and operational factors, but their determination, ingenuity and resourcefulness in providing a service of pin-point accuracy must be admired. At the height of the war over 7,000 men were employed; the Home Depot handled 2,000 million letters and papers, and moved 114 million parcels. The morale factor of an efficient postal service can never be underestimated; the Royal Engineers Postal Section had to cope with the demands of men who had volunteered or been called up from their homes. Unlike the professional soldiers, they and their families had not become hardened to long periods of separation and they maintained an enormous volume of correspondence.

War consumed men as well as supplies. As part of the massive effort to replace men in the depots, army kitchens, shell-filling factories and behind the wheels of cars and ambulances, more and more women were to be seen 'doing their bit' and demonstrating the validity of the suffragettes' claims to equality with men. The earliest women's organisation, the Women's Forage Corps, was attached to the Army Service Corps. Women drivers serving in the UK were initially attached to ASC MT (mechanical transport) companies before getting their own organisation, while women of the First Aid Nursing Yeomanry (FANY) drove ambulances in France and Belgium in an active service role. The vital work of women during the First World War did more for their emancipation than any suffragette movement on its own could have achieved,

and married women over the age of 30 finally received the vote in 1918.

As the complex alliances drew more and more nations into the conflict, the title of 'World War' became more appropriate. In addition to the pre-war outposts of the empire, the logistic services found themselves supporting armies in the Mediterranean, the Middle East, Africa, and from 1918, Russia. Abroad, the Army Service Corps and Ordnance Services provided essential support in Salonika, Gallipoli, East Africa, Mesopotamia, Egypt, Palestine, Italy and Russia. Each theatre produced its own problems and deserves its own account. The campaign in Mesopotamia was particularly noteworthy for the first use of aircraft to drop supplies to General Townshend's British and Indian forces besieged by the Turks at Kut-el-Amara in 1916.

Decorations and awards to individual members of all the corps are too numerous to mention, but of particular importance are the Victoria Crosses awarded to Second-Lieutenant Alfred Herring ASC and Private George Masters ASC in 1918. Second-Lieutenant Herring had been attached to 6th Battalion Northamptonshire Regiment, and commanded a post at Montagne Bridge, Jussy during Operation Michael, the first of the great German offensives known collectively as the *Kaiserschlacht* (Emperor's Battle). On 23 March 1918, two days after the start of the offensive, German forces, led by stormtroopers fresh from victories on the Eastern Front, gained a position on the south bank of the Crozat Canal after severe fighting. Herring and his men were cut off from friendly troops on both flanks and surrounded. Herring immediately led a counter-attack and recaptured the position, taking 20 prisoners and six machine-guns. He continued to exhort and inspire his men, constantly visiting them

What's on the menu today? *Female caterers at work in an army kitchen while soldiers peer in through the windows (at the food or the girls?), Boulogne, 1919. Painted by Sir John Lavery RA. The static nature of trench warfare in the First World War meant that on the Western Front it was possible to establish permanent kitchens in the support lines to the forward areas, in the rest areas further to the rear and throughout the lines of communications and base areas. From late 1915, responsibility for army catering lay with the Catering Section of the Army Service Corps. It was not until 1941, part way through another war, that the Army Catering Corps, a corps entirely dedicated to meeting the catering needs of the British Army, would be raised.*

under heavy fire. The German advance was held up for 11 hours at a critical period in the battle.

Private Masters was a driver attached to 141 Field Ambulance. On 9 April, at the beginning of the German Georgette offensive, British forces came under heavy attack at Bethune. Communications were cut off and wounded troops could not be evacuated. Although the road was reported impassable, Masters volunteered to try to restore contact, and after the greatest difficulty succeeded, although he had to clear the road of all sorts of debris. He made journey after journey throughout the afternoon, over a road frequently shelled and swept by machine-gun fire, and was on one occasion bombed by an aeroplane. Most of the wounded cleared from the area were evacuated by Masters, as his was the only ambulance that got through.

Ultimately co-operation between each branch of the logistic services was the key to success and each corps contributed enormously. The Army Ordnance Corps and Department had 240 officers and 2,300 men in 1914; during the war numbers grew to 2,400 officers and 39,000 men. The Army Service Corps began the war with 500 officers and 6,000 men and finished with 10,400 officers and 315,000 men, as well as 23,800 cars and vans, 56,600 lorries and tractors and 34,000 motor cycles. In recognition of their achievements, the Army Service Corps was granted the title 'Royal' on 25 November 1918, as were the Army Ordnance Department and Army Ordnance Corps on their amalgamation as the Royal Army Ordnance Corps.

THE INTER-WAR YEARS 1919–39

In the aftermath of the Great War the nation was exhausted. The Treasury had built up huge debts and industry was geared to supplying the voracious appetite of war. In spite of large scale demobilisation in 1919 the army still had commitments in many parts of the world, including the occupation of the Rhineland, which ended in 1929. The contraction of the economy to a peacetime footing hit everyone hard, not least because Britain was bankrupt, a situation which was not helped by a world depression.

The army was reduced to a level where, in addition to its occupation of areas of the Rhineland and North Russia, its continuing peacetime commitments in the West Indies, Turkey, Hong Kong, Egypt, the Sudan, India and Ireland could barely be met. The new League of Nations had given responsibility for the policing of troubled areas to certain member states, and this new task was to occupy large numbers of troops working in co-operation with the RAF in the Middle East. The Royal Army Service Corps and Royal Army Ordnance Corps were called upon to provide units for a host of peacetime emergencies: Turkey in 1922, Shanghai in 1927, Palestine in 1930, the Saar in 1934, and the Western Desert as a result of the Italian invasion of Abyssinia in 1935.

The logistic services were also given the task of dismantling the machinery of war. Recovery and subsequent reconditioning or disposal of equipment was to take many years. The army carried out these responsibilities while operating at subsistence level. The severe cuts which resulted from the infamous Geddes Committee, based on the premise of 'no major war for ten years', took their toll on morale. The Labour Corps was disbanded in 1919. The Army Postal Service was cut and, after the withdrawal of troops from Ireland and Turkey in the early 1920s, could only maintain a full service to the troops in Germany. Although the Postal Service remained with the British army of the Rhine, it was otherwise largely reduced to Supplementary Reserve status.

Under constant budgetary restraint, the logistic ser-

vices sought to apply the lessons of the war and the emerging technology to their specialist fields. The Royal Army Service Corps and Royal Army Ordnance Corps trialled and reported on an amazing variety of vehicles, seeking the ideal designs for fighting and support vehicles for the new mechanised army. The Army Postal Service, with the RAF, pioneered regular air mail

First Air Post: Folkestone-Köln by Terence Cuneo, March 1978. During 1918 experiments were carried out using modified aircraft for transporting the army's mail by air. As the tests proved successful, the first regular air service from Folkestone to Cologne (Köln) was set up in March 1919 to provide British troops in Germany with a fast mail service. This painting commemorates the first scheduled air mail from England to Germany. A de Havilland DH9 aircraft of the Royal Air Force, with its machine-gun removed, has its cargo of mail unloaded at Cologne and checked by a Corporal of the Royal Engineers Postal Section. Cologne cathedral can be seen in the background between the aircraft's wings.

flights to Germany. To enhance the professionalism of the logistic services, officers were sent on a variety of specialist courses, which included six-month-long attachments to the motor industry and administrative courses with the London School of Economics.

Horse transport units were reduced as mechanisation increased throughout the army. The Royal Army Service Corps' first purely mechanical transport station in peacetime was established at Feltham, combining the Heavy Repair Shop from Hounslow, the Driving School from Bulford, the MT Stores Depot from Deptford and the Vehicle Reserve Depot. The Royal Army Service Corps took over responsibility for training all drivers throughout the army and the Royal Army Ordnance Corps was made responsible in 1929 for the supply, storage and repair of all non-RASC vehicles and Other Arms' tracked and fighting vehicles. An experimental workshop was set up in Aldershot which, in the continuing quest for increased mobility, developed six-wheel trucks, as well as tracked and wheeled tractors to pull medium and heavy guns. In the 1930s a new Divisional Column RASC was created, comprising HQ, Supply, Ammunition and Baggage Companies, each company with its own mobile workshop section. Never before had such a complete and adequate transport system been designed to support the British army in the field.

After 1919 the headquarters of the Royal Army Ordnance Corps, together with the Depot, School of Instruction and Record Office, moved from Red Barracks, Woolwich to larger barracks at Hilsea near Portsmouth, where they remained until 1940. With increasing cuts and civilianisation, the Royal Army Ordnance Corps were driven back to the basic duty of providing the minimum needs of the army in peace, so that only a static organisation developed, with no up-

'Recruiting poster: Royal Army Ordnance Corps' by Ernest Ibbotson, inter-war years. The poster lists a variety of 'Trades and Callings' needed by the corps: clerks, storemen, carpenters, saddlers, blacksmiths, wheelers, fitters, painters, and tentmenders. During the 1920s and 1930s the British army found it very difficult to attract high quality recruits. After the First World War the army was seen as a huge cost to the nation and a reminder of horrors best forgotten. Soldiers' pay and conditions were poor and the army's reputation was damaged when soldiers were called upon to intervene in the strikes that spread across the land during the 1920s. The large pacifist movement that arose in Britain in the 1930s made re-arming against the threat of Nazi Germany all the more difficult.

to-date, tested Field Force organisation and no Regular Field Force units in peacetime. Its non-combatant status (later changed in 1941) again deterred progress.

In the 1930s, catering in the army was the subject of considerable attention in a drive to improve standards of living for the soldier. In 1938 Sir Isidore Salmon, Chairman of Lyons, a high street catering specialist, was invited by Leslie Hore-Belisha, the Secretary of State for War, to become Honorary Advisor on army catering. In 1939 the new School of Army Cookery was built opposite Clayton Barracks, Aldershot to replace the single block used in Buller Barracks since the end of the Great War. Civilian catering advisers were appointed in each of the Home Commands, and a new barracks, St Omer, the new School of Cookery, was established.

The American stock market crash of 1929, which spread economic depression throughout Europe, meant that spending on the armed forces remained desperately low. In Germany, however, the Depression provided a focus of resentment for the punitive 1919 Treaty of Versailles. Observers in Britain began to detect danger signs in the new concept of National Socialism, and in the early 1930s the 'no major war for ten years' policy was abandoned.

As British troops served with multi-national forces, the idea of rearmament was reborn. Unfortunately, finance was still not available to exploit all the experimentation and training carried out during the lean years. While the Spanish Civil War brought a vivid foretaste of modern warfare, RAOC workshops were hastily refurbishing 1914 rifles for the coming conflict.

THE SECOND WORLD WAR 1939–45

'The outcome of any battle is decided before the first shot has been fired – by the Quartermaster!'
Field Marshal Erwin Rommel

In 1938 the British government finally began serious preparations for war as Prime Minister Neville Chamberlain's influence on Hitler proved to be illusory. Militia men reported for duty and the process of mobilisation started. In 1939 the Territorial Army was embodied and National Service introduced; the 'impressed vehicle' scheme was put into operation and a variety of civilian vehicles were hurriedly painted khaki. Transport, Ordnance and Pioneer units came rapidly into being, the latter initially called the 'Auxiliary Military Pioneer Corps' (changed a year later to the Pioneer Corps). Unfortunately, when

Chamberlain announced to the nation in 1939 that Britain was at war with Germany, the army was not ready, even though its equipment was modern and new techniques were being taught.

BLITZKRIEG 1939–40

Only 25 years after its predecessor in 1914, another British Expeditionary Force embarked for France, where, during the lull known as the 'phoney war', the logistic services encountered once more the difficulties of the Great War. The tactical and logistic situations were in many ways comparable, only this time the German army was significantly more successful, completely defeating the French army in under six weeks during May 1940. The BEF also suffered against the *blitzkrieg* tactics of the Germans, and in June the harried remnants of the British army had to be evacuated through Dunkirk. With many examples of individual gallantry, the troops retreated across the Channel. The logistic services, having worked hard to provide supplies in the field, establish lines of communication and construct defensive positions and airfields, had to abandon their efforts, taking only mobile equipment and destroying what remained. Many Corps soldiers were captured and remained prisoners-of-war until 1945.

As the army struggled to reorganise and re-equip in Britain, the logistic services found themselves playing new roles in the coming air battles. Airfield defences and repair, support to the many anti-aircraft batteries and, as the bombing became a dreadful reality, clearing rubble from bombed areas and lighting oil fires to confuse the bombers were some of the tasks undertaken during the Battle of Britain. The equipment lost in France, in addition to being replaced, had to be re-designed to incorporate the lessons of defeat. Each new theatre of war brought more changes. The burden of re-building the army was immense.

Industry was again geared to make good the losses and, as in the Great War, women were mobilised not only for work in the factories, but also in uniform. Thousands of members of the new Auxiliary Territorial Service (ATS) worked with the logistic services, releasing men for service overseas.

Royal Army Service Corps

The Royal Army Service Corps expanded greatly during the Second World War: 10,000-strong in 1939, it rose to 325,000 men in 1945. One soldier in every ten wore the Royal Army Service Corps badge, and the corps' achievements, like its numbers, were enormous. As with its sister corps, the Royal Army Service Corps was directed from a number of Supply and Transport Branches in the War Office. The corps was fortunate in the quality and experience of its officers, and provided the first head of corps of the REME on its formation in 1942, Major-General Bertram Rowcroft. Wherever the army served there were units of the Royal Army Service Corps and, with its staff clerks in most embassies throughout the world, the corps was also represented where there were no other units.

While the 3-ton truck was the main work-horse of the corps in all theatres, there were a number of interesting developments in other forms of transport and supply. The composite ration was introduced for the Norway expedition in 1940, for example, and then developed over the next few years so that soldiers had a choice of menu. Pack transport was used in difficult terrain, in France in 1940 by the Royal Indian Army Service Corps, and later in North Africa, Sicily and Italy. When German stocks of petrol were captured in North Africa in 1940, the German container was found to be far superior to the old British 'flimsie' and the 'jerrycan' quickly replaced it. In the North African desert the vast distances, the nature of the terrain and the mechanised aspect of the conflict brought new problems, such as the need to transport fresh water and to deploy armour over long distances. Tank transporters were used on a large scale for the first time and came into their own on long hauls along the North African coastline. The units which supplied and repaired the fighting vehicles had to become much more mobile. American trucks were preferred, as were their tank transporters. In the latter case, the Diamond T models were delivered direct from America to the 8th Army.

The Evacuation from Dunkirk in 1940, by C. Cundall. The escape of the bulk of the British Expeditionary Force from France gave Britain a core of experienced soldiers around which to rebuild the field army. The logistic services suffered a serious blow, however, when one of the troopships taking part in the evacuation, the Lancastria, *was sunk with heavy loss of life. Most of the troops on board were from the Royal Army Service Corps and the Royal Army Ordnance Corps.*

Painting of British tank transporters in North Africa, 1942, by David Cobb in 1984. 144 Company (TT) RASC was the first tank transporter unit to be deployed to North Africa. During the withdrawal to the Gazala Line early in 1942 Captain W. M. Nichol of 144 Company, in command of 21 vehicles, managed to recover 12 tanks and crews while under heavy fire from enemy tanks and artillery. The British Grant tanks were loaded onto the transporters, facing backwards to enable their hull-mounted main guns to continue firing during the withdrawal. Captain Nichol was awarded the DSO for this action.

Although there were two recorded occasions in the Great War when supplies or ammunition were dropped from aircraft (Kut el Amara and Arras), air despatch was first used extensively in Burma, led by the Royal Indian Army Service Corps. Air transport provided a vital life-line in the effort to resupply British and Commonwealth troops fighting the Japanese, and established a close link with the Royal Air Force which has continued ever since.

Moving supplies and mail, perhaps more important than ever in the strange and hazardous environment of the jungle, also called for an increased reliance on light vehicles and animal transport. In Europe, efforts by air despatchers to supply surrounded airborne troops at Arnhem in September 1944 led to heavy casualties and a reputation second-to-none for determination and gallantry.

The amphibious wheeled transport vehicles known as DUKWs proved invaluable in Italy 1943–44 and more widely throughout north-west Europe. Less well-known but equally important was their use in Burma, largely on the River Irrawaddy, where they were also used as assault craft. Water transport supply was critical to allied success during the war, generally in British waters but also in the Mediterranean, particularly during the siege of Malta in 1942 when every vessel was hit by enemy fire.

There were many examples of bravery among the personnel of the Royal Army Service Corps Fleet: the last boat to leave the beaches of Dunkirk in 1940 was the RASC vessel *Marlborough*, which left under tow, both her propellers having been blown off; and in 1944 RASC Fleet vessels took part in the D-Day landings, dodging mines off Normandy and rescuing men from a part of the Mulberry harbour which was breaking up in a storm.

ROYAL ARMY ORDNANCE CORPS

The Royal Army Ordnance Corps played a major and essential part in the Second World War. Starting with a nucleus of a few hundred officers and a few thousand men of the Regular and Territorial Army, the corps developed in little more than four years into an efficient organisation of 8,000 officers and 130,000 men. From the Ordnance Directorate in the War Office, which dealt with policy, corps organisation world-wide and the provision of stores, vehicles and ammunition, a UK base was created to supply all items of Ordnance concern to all theatres. This was complemented by a smaller base in the Middle East and a comprehensive Field Force organisation which pro-vided a reliable and flexible system for the maintenance of a Field Army, including Ordnance Field Parks, Forward Maintenance Ammunition Sections, Forward Maintenance Stores Sections, Mobile Laundry and Bath Units, Mobile Ammunition Repair Units, Ordnance Beach Detachments and Industrial Gas Units.

Base and Lines of Communication units in theatres of operations were Base Ordnance Depots, Base Ammunition Depots, Vehicle Depots, Base and Hospital Laundries, Base Industrial Gas Units, Port Ordnance and Ammunition Detachments. The war saw the creation of a large workshop organisation for the repair, recovery and manufacture of a large range of equipment at the base and in the field, which was trans-ferred on the creation of the Royal Electrical and Mechanical Engineers in 1942.

Within this variety of services the changing face of warfare demanded considerable flexibility. The UK depot organisation became, in some cases unwillingly, the largest employers of the new Auxiliary Territorial

Service (ATS), introducing women to a variety of tasks employing the latest techniques in mechanical handling and card-based information technology. In the field, units which had previously come to rely on static locations had to develop new techniques and equipment to become mobile.

As the war spread throughout the world, the Royal Army Ordnance Corps became world leaders in packing stores to protect them from the ravages of varied climates. In the Far East, for example, operations in the harsh jungle conditions took their toll not only of men's health, but also of their clothing and equipment. It was in this particularly trying environment in January 1944 that an Ordnance Divisional Sub-park distinguished itself in an infantry role. Located on the Burma border, the sub-park held off a series of heavy Japanese attacks for 17 days while issuing stores to surrounding units under extremely difficult circumstances.

In general, Ordnance success in the war was based on the integration of staffs and commands at all levels, which had never been achieved before. Together with a close and direct control from Whitehall, this enabled the Royal Army Ordnance Corps to supply the fighting troops with ever-increasing needs in arms, equipment and ammunition, whether tackling the acute shortages early on or dealing with the complicated and ambitious projects later in the war.

PIONEER CORPS

Pioneers performed a wide variety of tasks in the UK and in every theatre of war. Many were recruited from around the empire: East and West Africa, Swaziland, Basutoland, Bechuanaland, Mauritius and India. Companies established with Beach Groups took part in the assaults in North Africa, Sicily and Italy. In north-west Europe on D-Day, 26 companies, totalling 7,500 men, landed on the Normandy beaches. By D+60 they were followed by 34 Group HQs and a further 205 companies totalling 60,000 men. They worked on the beaches, laid prefabricated track, handled all types of stores and ammunition and carried out stretcher-bearing and road-making duties. With Engineer supervision other companies built the Mulberry harbour, laid the Pipe Line Under the Ocean (PLUTO), constructed airfields and erected bridges. Strategic and tactical smoke screens were laid by Pioneers, who also supplied the smoke cover for the crossing of the Rhine.

At most operational ports and railheads, Pioneers were responsible for all non-technical labour, and they were often able to take over technical tasks without supervision. Companies were also trained to fight and took their place in the line as Infantry in Tunisia. Less spectacular, but nevertheless essential, were the Lines of Communication and Base tasks performed overseas and in the UK. Millions of tons of stores were handled for the services at all stages of transit. Pioneers became expert in loading and unloading railway waggons and motor transport. Pioneer and Civil Labour Units (PCLUs) recruited civilians as close to the fighting as possible, thus relieving the strain on the military Pioneer. These units were particularly successful in recruiting skilled artisans and clerks for the Royal Engineers, Royal Army Ordnance Corps and Royal Electrical and Mechanical Engineers units, as well as a large number of unskilled workers.

It was an enormous world-wide commitment, which may be fairly judged from the fact that in 1945 the Pioneer Corps included 12,000 officers and controlled the following numbers of men: 166,000 uniformed Pioneers, 330,000 labourers from a variety of countries in the Empire, 1,074,000 civilian labour and

Pioneers. Sword Beach. D-Day Normandy. Painted by Terence Cuneo, February 1993, when aged 83. Sword Beach was administered by 101 Beach Sub-Area, in which 5 and 9 Beach Groups operated. Each Beach Group was assigned a force of Pioneers, whose first task was to clear mines and underwater obstacles. Other tasks included unloading landing craft, building ammunition and other dumps, constructing beach tracks to carry the guns, armour and miscellaneous vehicles to the firm land beyond, collection and evacuation of the wounded, collection and burial of the dead, guarding prisoners-of-war and, if necessary, joining the assault forces in the battle.

173,000 prisoner-of-war labour, all officered and staffed by the Pioneer Corps, a grand total of 1,743,000 men.

ARMY CATERING CORPS

Early in the war a determined effort was made to tackle the weaknesses of military catering. The Army Catering Corps was formed on 22 March 1941 by Special Order 35 in order to provide a professional focus and continued training. The first Director was effectively Colonel R. A. A. Byford, then Deputy-Director Supplies and Transport, ST 4 (Catering) in the War Office. A School of Cookery was established at Aldershot in the same year, and Sir Isidore Salmon, Chairman of Lyons, was made Honorary Catering Adviser to the Army. The first Commandant ACC Training Centre in the new St Omer Barracks, where the corps formed, was Lieutenant-Colonel R. Russell. Sir Isidore Salmon was followed in 1959 as Honorary Catering Adviser to the army by his nephew, Geoffrey Salmon, who was in turn succeeded in 1971 by his son, Harry Salmon. During the war the corps became a highly successful organisation and included a great number of civilian catering experts who were called up 'for the duration'. Some 70,000 officers and men served in the Army Catering Corps during the war. On 5 October 1945 the Army Council took the decision to retain the corps as an integral part of the post-war army.

ROYAL ENGINEERS POSTAL SECTION

The Postal Section of the Royal Engineers was authorised on 24 August 1939, ten days before the outbreak of war. The Mount Pleasant Sorting Office in London swung into action, but it was not long before safety considerations (the threat of bombing) led to a move to Reading, then later to Bournemouth and Nottingham. Once again, the Postal Service battled with the problems of unit locations, or rather lack of information on them. Probably the most important postal innovation of the war was the 'airgraph', a Kodak idea, which eventually evolved into the air letter. Introduced in May 1941, they were light and used minimal space in aircraft, leading to a notable improvement in mail from the Middle East. Letters and addresses written on special forms were photographed and rolls of negatives were sent to Britain by air. Once there, positive prints of the films were made, smaller than the original forms, which were then posted free in windowed envelopes, through normal postal channels.

Postal arrangements in North Africa were perhaps typical: at the end of the campaign in 1943 there were 53 British Army Post Offices serving the Lines of Communication areas, and 36 British Army Post Offices with operational formations. The Base Army Post Office in Cairo was the centre of this organisation. The war in the Western Desert involved frequent advances and retreats over long distances, and provided a searching test for the Army Postal Service. In the fluid battles, when even corps and divisional HQs were overrun by German forces, postal units had their moments of excitement and share of casualties.

For the attack on Europe in 1944 a new 'closed address' system was introduced which would not only obviate security problems at a time when the point of landing was a closely-guarded secret, but would also be easier to handle. As the Allies moved through France, Belgium and Holland, postal roadheads moved forward into Germany and airfields were brought into use as they were captured, thus allowing the mail service to achieve the highest standards in supporting the army. After 1945, during the period of demobilisation, German and Belgian civilians provided invaluable assistance. Fortunately, the army appeared to have learnt from past mistake, and there was no question of the Postal Service becoming a Reserve Force again.

LIBERATION OF EUROPE 1944-45

In Europe, as the allied forces fighting in Africa moved to Italy, the corps gained valuable experience in the use of landing craft and amphibious vehicles. This knowledge was soon applied in the D-Day landings. The preparations had been immense. Under a veil of secrecy southern England became a huge holding area for troops, equipment and supplies. On 6 June 1944 the first troops landed in Normandy. Men of the logistic services accompanied them to provide direct support under fire. The continued logistical support of the soldiers fighting their way in a bitter campaign through Europe was an operation of a size which has never been equalled. Depots in Britain collected and dispatched huge volumes of material to the docks. On the other side of the Channel the supplies were taken ashore by DUKWs or landing craft, sometimes operating in fierce storms, and over the huge Mulberry harbour which was built in southern England. Ordnance Beach Detachments landed ammunition under difficult circumstances. A postal service was provided from the beachhead and, accompanying the units fighting to clear the beachhead, members of the Army Catering Corps improvised hot meals. To provide the vast quantities of fuel needed for the campaign, a pipe-line was laid under the Channel.

As the fighting moved through Europe, the vital lines of communication were stretched. The rapid movement of units meant that those providing supplies, mail and maintenance had first to find units and then keep up with them. Air dispatch proved vital in the support of airborne operations, most notably in the Netherlands during Operation Market Garden in September 1944, when the British 30 Corps and British and American airborne troops attempted to seize a series of river bridges, culminating in the attack on the bridge over the Rhine at Arnhem. Both Royal Army Service Corps and Royal Army Ordnance Corps units helped defend the Oosterbeek perimeter to the bitter end, fighting side by side with the paratroopers of 1st Airborne Division, until they were finally defeated by German armoured formations.

In early 1945, with the Rhine still to be crossed, the support and movement of bridging units became a priority, together with the movement of landing craft and DUKWs from the coast. The Wehrmacht and SS formations fought fanatically to defend Germany and, as in the Great War, soldiers were frequently taken from the logistic services to replace casualties in British front line fighting units.

POST-WAR YEARS 1945-93

As in 1919, the period of transition from war to peace was difficult. The end of the Second World War in 1945 should have brought peace, but occupation duties and other world-wide commitments in the final years of the empire saw British forces extensively involved in a series of brush fire wars. The army maintained a presence in British colonies throughout the world, areas policed by Britain during the inter-war years and territories occupied during the Second World War. As Britain sought to withdraw from these areas and to allow a gradual change to independent government, troops were frequently caught up in conflicts between rival groups. In Malaya, Borneo, Palestine, Aden and Cyprus the army spent many years under fire, keeping the peace or providing stability for an emerging regime.

Continuing world-wide commitments allowed the logistic services to develop their various roles. Guided missiles, computers and hovercraft provided new challenges (the RAOC's first portable computer needed a 3-ton truck to carry it), while in colonial and post-colonial conflicts throughout the world servicemen appreciated the efforts of the Postal Service and the increasingly professional Army Catering Corps.

With the presence in Europe of Russian and American armies, the age of the superpower dawned. The balance of world politics was to be dominated by the manoeuvring of East and West, and increasingly Britain's role as a world power reduced. The first emergency of what became known as the Cold War came to a head with the Russian blockade of Berlin in 1948. The British army's logistic services were heavily involved in Operation Plainfare, the huge air supply operation launched to enable Berlin to survive until the Russians lifted the blockade. From 1949 British troops occupying Germany were to become part of the first line of defence within the North Atlantic Treaty Organisation (NATO). In Korea (1950–53) and the Suez (1956), troops found themselves fighting in local conflicts dominated by superpower ambitions.

As the Cold War continued, military thinking was increasingly dominated by the threat of nuclear power. Soldiers were now required to understand the basic theories of nuclear, biological and chemical warfare and regularly trained to operate wearing uncomfortable protective clothing (NBC suits). In the late 1960s Britain's world-wide commitment diminished; the army concentrated its efforts on the NATO presence in Germany and, increasingly, the troubles in Northern Ireland. Development within the British army continued, however, in the search to improve and inevitably to do more with less.

ROYAL ARMY SERVICE CORPS/
ROYAL CORPS OF TRANSPORT

In 1951 the Royal Army Service Corps lost its remaining unit workshops to the Royal Electrical and Mechanical Engineers. In 1957 the armoured transport regiment role went to the Royal Armoured Corps, although the Royal Corps of Transport (formed in 1965) effectively took on the latter role in Northern Ireland with great efficiency. Post-war losses in the Royal Corps of Transport continued with the disband-

18 Transport Squadron RNZCT in Rubber Plantations, Malaysia, by Ian Brown. The painting was presented by the Royal New Zealand Corps of Transport to mark the formation of The Royal Logistic Corps in April 1993. In 1964 a two-year-old Indonesian-backed insurrection in the British Borneo territories became a 'confrontation' between Indonesia and the newly created Malaysian Federation, which lasted until 1966. In early 1965, in accordance with their obligations as members of the South East Asia Treaty Organisation (SEATO), Australian and New Zealand forces began to deploy in Borneo alongside the British troops already involved in the conflict. The 3-ton Bedford lorries depicted in the painting were the workhorse of the Royal Army Service Corps (Royal Corps of Transport from 1965) and its counterparts in the Commonwealth throughout the 1950s and 1960s.

ment of the Bridging Regiment in 1970 when M2 bridges were introduced. The Longmoor Railway was closed in 1969 and the last horse transport companies in the UK and in Hong Kong were disbanded in 1970 and 1976 respectively. Responsibility for aircraft liaison flights ended in 1970 and the hovercraft squadron was disbanded in 1974; the venerable DUKW, a 32-year-old amphibian craft, was withdrawn from service at the same time. The air despatch organisation was reduced, so that only one regular squadron and a Territorial Army troop remained to keep the requisite skills alive, skills that were frequently and urgently called upon throughout the world. Air despatch was used to render humanitarian assistance during the 1980s and 1990s in Zimbabwe, Nepal, Ethiopia and Iraq, to mention but four occasions.

ROYAL ARMY ORDNANCE CORPS

In 1948 the Royal Army Ordnance Corps moved to Deepcut. Its headquarters had moved several times during the war, so it was reassuring to settle in such a pleasant area, especially since this move allowed the concentration of the HQ Training Centre, the Depot and Training Battalion, the School of Ordnance and the Apprentices College. The corps' position in the army was greatly enhanced by its tremendous contribution to the war effort; at last commanders and staffs in the War Office and elsewhere seemed to have learnt from history and Royal Army Ordnance Corps officers and men took their place as respected equals in the army.

Explosive Ordnance Disposal was a particularly important responsibility of the Royal Army Ordnance Corps, an area of activity valued and appreciated by the army and general public alike. Involvement in Cyprus, Aden and Hong Kong in the 1950s was followed by a major effort in Northern Ireland from the late 1960s. Close liaison with the Royal Ulster Constabulary and units on the ground, coupled with the introduction of sophisticated equipment, notably the 'Wheelbarrow', resulted in frequent frustration for the terrorists and saved many lives and much property. Recognition of this gallant work could be seen in the award of six George Crosses and 67 George Medals to EOD personnel since 1940.

ROYAL PIONEER CORPS

In 1946 the Pioneer Corps was granted the title 'Royal' in recognition of its very valuable work during the years 1939–45. Like all other corps, however, it was much reduced in size after the war, but still retained extensive commitments. Unlike the Great War of 1914–18, the corps was retained as part of the permanent post-war Regular Army and was honoured in June 1977 with the appointment of HRH The Duke of Gloucester as Colonel-in-Chief. The Corps HQ occupied several locations during the Second World War and their travels ceased only in September 1960 when they moved to Quebec Barracks, Northampton (renamed Simpson Barracks in 1961).

ARMY CATERING CORPS

In 1945, having reached a strength of 70,000 during the war, the Army Catering Corps remained in the Order of Battle and was therefore able to continue the improvements initiated by Sir Isidore Salmon. The key was the introduction of apprenticeships, started in 1947, which led to the creation of a corps of top class tradesmen who can hold their own anywhere in the world of catering.

From simple beginnings in 1937–38 with regimental cooks at the Hotel Olympia, to the present day, army chefs have been outstandingly successful, and the corps built a reputation as one of the leading organisations in British catering. Prime Ministers' conferences, Commonwealth leaders' meetings, Chequers weekends and a number of embassy functions have all involved Army Catering Corps chefs, and in 1992 the Corps took part in the German International Food Fair in Frankfurt.

ROYAL ENGINEERS POSTAL AND COURIER SERVICE

The Postal Services became involved with NATO headquarters in the early 1950s, and gradually, from

The Berlin Military Train, painted by Ken Howard. The Royal Corps of Transport took over responsibility for military railways, including the Berlin Military Train, from the Royal Engineers in 1965. The day-to-day running of the Berlin Military Train was controlled by 486 Movements Troop RCT, then, from 1971, 62 Transport and Movements Squadron RCT (Berlin). The train left Charlottenburg station, Berlin, at 0849 hours daily, carrying British and allied servicemen and their families out of Berlin, either on duty or on leave visits. The operation of military railways is now the responsibility of The Royal Logistic Corps. RLC soldiers operated the Kosovo railway system in 1999.

The British Military Train

A Lull in the Battle, painted by Terence Cuneo, September 1984. The painting was commissioned by the Headquarters Officers' Mess, Army Catering Corps, and handed over to The Royal Logistic Corps on 2 July 1997 by the ACC Trust Council. It depicts soldiers of the Army Catering Corps providing hot food and tea for men of 2nd Battalion The Parachute Regiment during the Falklands War, 1982. During the bitter fighting in the latter days of the war, as well as carrying out normal cookhouse duties, ACC personnel worked for 36 hours non-stop as stretcher-bearers and ammunition-carriers. Four out of the 12 ACC cooks attached to 2nd Battalion The Parachute Regiment were killed in action on 8 June 1982.

1953 took on the transmission of classified mails world-wide. In 1962 the Home Postal Depot moved from Acton to Mill Hill in London, its present location and, having previously accepted responsibility for RAF mails, took over HM ships' mail from the Post Office, thus becoming both a tri-service and an international military service.

After further developments and changes of name, in July 1992 the Minister of State for the Armed Forces launched the Defence Postal and Courier Services Defence Support Agency at Mill Hill. This status allowed the Royal Engineers Postal and Courier Service in the UK to operate along more commercial lines, to streamline its operation and expand its entrepreneurial activities within a specified budget from the government.

THE MCLEOD COMMITTEE

In March 1963 the Army Council set up a committee under General Sir Roderick McLeod to review the efficiency of the existing Logistic Services of the British army. The recommendations of the McLeod Committee prompted a number of changes in 1965 which affected several corps and paved the way towards the creation of The Royal Logistic Corps in 1993. The three great Quartermaster-General Services, namely the Royal Army Service Corps, Royal Army Ordnance Corps and Royal Electrical and Mechanical Engineers, overlapped in many ways, particularly as regards provisioning, stores holding and transport management and control. It was decided that the Royal Army Service Corps should become the transport and distribution corps of the army, taking over railways, port operations and movement control from the Royal Engineers.

Responsibility for supply and fuel provisioning and stores holding, the Fire Service, Barrack Services and Staff Clerks was transferred from the Royal Army Service Corps to the Royal Army Ordnance Corps. Meanwhile, the Royal Army Ordnance Corps took over the provision of Royal Engineers plant and machinery. Whereas the Royal Army Service Corps had its name changed to the Royal Corps of Transport, its ninth change in 200 years, the Royal Army Ordnance Corps, as the army's provisioning and stores-holding Corps, escaped the implementation of General McLeod's recommendation that it should be renamed 'The Supply Corps', to everyone's relief.

GLOBAL RESPONSE

The wealth of technology available to military planners might have appeared to have undermined the role of the field soldier. In 1982 and 1991, however, the invasion of the Falklands by Argentina and the war against Iraq in the Gulf were timely reminders that there can be no substitute for the soldier on the ground, who must be well-supported anywhere in the world. The 1990s brought new pressures to the logistic services. With the end of the Cold War, the government demanded significant reductions in defence spending and the army was reduced, but still kept most of its commitments. Fewer troops were required in Germany, but peacekeeping and humanitarian operations throughout the world offered new challenges. Throughout the services, units were disbanded or amalgamated. Within the world of logistics, the Royal Corps of Transport, Royal Army Ordnance Corps, Royal Pioneer Corps, Army Catering Corps and the Royal Engineers Postal and Courier Service were amalgamated to form The Royal Logistic Corps on

(RIGHT) The Royal Corps of Transport in action during the Gulf War, February 1991, *painted by Anthony Cowland. The painting depicts 27 Regiment RCT moving forward in support of the British advance into Kuwait against the Iraqi occupiers in Operation Desert Storm. The Gulf War involved the largest operational deployment of British armour since the Second World War, in the form of 1 (UK) Armoured Division. The corresponding deployment of RCT units in support was equally impressive, including 1 Armoured Divisional Transport Regiment, 4 Armoured Divisional Transport Regiment, 10 Regiment, 27 Regiment, 7 Tank Transporter Regiment, 50 and 59 Movement Control Squadrons, 52 Port Squadron and the Gurkha Ambulance Support Group.*

ABOVE Gulf War Montage *by C. R Anthony, 1992. The painting was one of three commissioned from different artists to celebrate the part played by the Royal Army Ordnance Corps to Operation Granby, the British contribution to Operation* Desert Storm. *The centrepiece shows 31 Ordnance Company, part of 3 Ordnance Battalion RAOC, loading Challenger gun barrels. The insignia to the right are, clockwise: the Kuwaiti national flag, 3 Ordnance Battalion, 1 UK Armoured* Division, 4 Armoured Brigade, the Force Maintenance Area (various FMA camps in Al Jubayl had been named after characters in the 'Blackadder' television series, hence the adoption of a black adder as the insignia) and 7 Armoured Brigade.

Formation Parade 5 April 1993. Commemorating the formation of The Royal Logistic Corps, *painted by Joan Wanklyn, 1993. The formation of The Royal Logistic Corps was marked by parades in various parts of the UK and abroad, but the central Formation Day Parade was held in Deepcut, attended by the Colonel-in-Chief, HRH The Princess Royal. The re-badging ceremony involved representative soldiers from each of the forming corps. Some 500 men were on parade, commanded by Lieutenant-Colonel R. Elliott, and accompanied by the Staff Band of The RLC which played the Corps march 'On Parade'. The parade was attended by 800 spectators and was covered by radio, television and the local and national press.*

5 April 1993. For the first time, units whose predecessors had in the past provided invaluable support to the soldier were united in what has become the largest corps in the British army.

LOGISTICS IN THE 1990s AND BEYOND

In the early years of its existence The Royal Logistic Corps has been continually engaged in operations across the world, providing vital support to the British army, and in some cases contributing the majority of troops to British forces deployed on active service overseas. Men and women of the corps have been involved around the globe as the cutting edge of humanitarian aid in support of the UN's efforts to keep the peace. As the war-torn 20th century drew to a close, the corps contributed to the maintenance of the uneasy peace in Northern Ireland and has been committed to UN and NATO operations in Bosnia, Rwanda, Angola, Kosovo, East Timor, Sierra Leone and Mozambique.

(RIGHT) *Painting by Johnny Jonas, 1999, showing a DROPS (Demountable Rack Off-Loading and Pick-Up System) convoy leaving 'Dalton Camp', Kupres, Bosnia-Herzegovina, in mid-winter. Both Close Support and General Support Regiments are equipped with DROPS vehicles, which entered service at the beginning of the 1990s. The flat rack can carry 15 tons of NATO pallets or unit loads and was developed to increase the total vehicle lift capacity for ammunition and explosives. The painting was commissioned by the officers of 3 Close Support Regiment RLC to mark the contribution of 3 Close Support Regiment and 4 General Support Regiment to British peace-keeping operations in the Former Republic of Yugoslavia since October 1993.*

Bosnia

The end of the Cold War and the decline of Communism as a world ideology left a political and spiritual vacuum in Eastern Europe. Nationalism, often inspired by centuries of ethnic hatred and temporarily suppressed by the Soviet Union, frequently filled the gap. In Yugoslavia, the absence of a strong leader following the death of President Tito in 1980 led to increasing hostility between the various states that comprised the republic. The election of Slobodan Milosevic as President of Serbia in 1987 resulted in a strongly nationalist Serbian foreign policy, at the expense of Serbia's Slovene, Croatian and Bosnian neighbours. When The Royal Logistic Corps was formed, the British army had been heavily committed in former Yugoslavia for almost a year as part of a multi-national effort to restrain the murderous policy of 'ethnic cleansing' practised by all sides. Units of the various forming corps had been deployed to the Balkans first in Croatia (Operation Hanwood, from April 1992), then in Bosnia (Operation Grapple, November 1992). These units were brigaded together as the National Support Element (NSE), with the role of supporting the British UNPROFOR contingent.

After the formation of The Royal Logistic Corps, 4 General Support Regiment RLC was deployed to Yugoslavia as part of Operation Grapple III and became the first of a number of RLC Support Regiments to form the core of the British Logistic Battalion (BRITLOGBAT), replacing the NSE. The British Logistic Battalion's function was to provide the support needed by the British forces in Bosnia to carry out their peace-keeping role. Their tasks included the re-supply of all stores, food, fuel, ammunition and other essential items required by British troops in the Balkans. These arrived by road or ship into the UN docks run by the battalion at the port of Split in Croatia, and were then transported by road into the British camps in central Bosnia. The British Logistic Battalion also supplied medical personnel and military police as well as the equipment support needed to keep the fleets of vehicles operating. It included a postal service and a labour support unit that employed local civilians to work for the UN.

At the end of 1995, as a result of the relative success of the Dayton Peace Agreement, Britain mounted Operation Resolute. A significantly larger force (including an armoured brigade) was sent to Bosnia as part of a larger NATO operation and required the commitment of a correspondingly greater number of Royal Logistic Corps formations. In Bosnia, as elsewhere, Royal Logistic Corps soldiers have sometimes had to perform infantry duties as well as fulfilling their own specialist roles. In 1998, for example, the Drivers and Supply Specialists of 2 (UK) Logistic Regiment were formed into an infantry platoon to take over the security of a large area of southern Bosnia. The platoon carried out foot and Land Rover patrols during a changeover between Malaysian and Belgian-Luxembourg battle groups, and closed down three illegal militia camps. At the time of writing, a significant British presence is still maintained in Bosnia, requiring a constant rotation of units from The Royal Logistic Corps to provide the necessary logistic support.

Rwanda

On 6 April 1994 the aircraft carrying the Hutu President Habyarimana of the ancient African kingdom of Rwanda and the President of Burundi was shot down. Thirty years of sporadic violence between the majority Hutu tribe and the originally highly privileged minority Tutsi tribe immediately exploded into open and bloody civil war. The exiled Tutsi Rwandan Patriotic Front (RPF) invaded the country, while Hutu militia practised systematic genocide, slaughtering Tutsi and moderate Hutu. The RPF took Kigali, the capital of Rwanda, on 6 July 1994. Thousands of Hutu fled the country, fearful of reprisals from the new Tutsi government, taking with them a depleted and embittered Hutu army that threatened to start the civil war all over again.

Vast refugee camps were established on both sides of the Rwanda–Zaire border. Conditions in these camps deteriorated rapidly, with cholera killing hundreds each day. The UN monitors already present in Rwanda were powerless to deal with the violence spreading throughout the country; accordingly, the UN Security Council issued a new mandate to provide for peacekeeping and humanitarian support. This involved deploying an Assistance Mission of 5,500 troops to Rwanda. Britain's contribution amounted to a force of over 600 soldiers, the nucleus of which was formed by 5 Airborne Brigade Logistic Battalion and 23 Parachute Field Ambulance RAMC. Britain had, in fact, been asked to provide as soon as possible specific support to tackle a number of medical, engineering and logistic problems facing the UN in a situation rapidly growing worse every day.

The contribution of The Royal Logistic Corps to the British contingent (BRITCON) deployed to Rwanda in July 1994 (Operation Gabriel) included 63 Airborne Close Support Squadron, 82 Airborne General Support Squadron, a Movements Detachment and a Postal and Courier Detachment, the last two from 29 Regiment. Lack of transport had been a serious problem as many UN vehicles had been abandoned or destroyed during the fighting. Britain therefore donated 50 4-ton Bedford trucks to the UN mission in Rwanda, which were operated in often difficult and treacherous terrain by 63 Airborne Close Support Squadron. The squadron were mainly involved in the movements of refugees from the camps on the Rwanda–Zaire border to their homes in Rwanda, while 82 Airborne General Support Squadron, based in Kigali, were responsible for maintaining the British contingent. When the British deployment came to an end three months later, these vehicles were left behind in Rwanda for the use of the UN.

Among the many contributions made by Royal Logistic Corps soldiers to the UN mission in Rwanda was assisting 23 Parachute Field Ambulance in setting up a hospital in the town of Ruhengeri. Corps personnel also took part in Operation Hedgehog, the mass vaccination of 45,600 refugees against meningitis over a four-day period. Soldiers from all units of BRITCON also gave of their scarce spare time to refurbish and restore power and sanitation to a number of Rwandan orphanages. The British contingent as a whole won praise and respect not only from other UN contingents, but also from the various relief agencies, for their extreme compassion towards the refugees and their commitment to rebuilding the infrastructure of a shattered country.

NORTHERN IRELAND

The most significant development in Northern Ireland since the formation of The Royal Logistic Corps was the first of a number of ceasefires declared by the Republican and Loyalist paramilitaries in late 1994. There was an immediate reduction in the number of bomb and shooting incidents in the province. In the 12 months leading up to the ceasefire over 1,400 such incidents occurred; five months after the declaration the number had dropped to less than 30. The result was a dramatic fall in the operational workload of the bomb disposal teams of 321 Explosive Ordnance Disposal Squadron. 321 EOD Squadron, the most decorated unit in the British army for actions undertaken in peace-time, celebrated 25 years of active service in Northern Ireland on 19 November 1996.

ANGOLA

On 8 February 1995 the UN Security Council passed Resolution 976 committing a force to the west African country of Angola, with the aim of actively seeking a permanent peace between the Angolan government and rebel UNITA forces. The British contribution (BRITFOR) to the UN force consisted mainly of Royal Logistic Corps units, 9 Supply Regiment, 17 Port & Maritime Regiment, 23 Pioneer Regiment and 29 Regiment. During the British deployment (Operation Chantress) most RLC troops were based at the port of Lobito, with the aim of assisting the deployment of UN troops as and when they arrived. In fact the flow of UN troops from other nations turned out to be much slower than expected. As a result, RLC personnel took advantage of the links established with local government and the local population and looked for opportunities to assist in educational and other projects that would improve the quality of life for ordinary Angolans, whose country had been riven by civil war for many years. Troops were soon painting and decorating classroom walls and improving the local water supply. In Operation Chantress, The Royal Logistic Corps had once again provided its expertise in an out-of-area operation.

KOSOVO

In early 1999 the savage conflict between the various ethnic peoples of the Balkans spilled over into Kosovo. The majority of Kosovans are Albanian Muslims and wished to secede from Serbia. The Serbian army attacked the Kosovan Albanians on the grounds that the minority Serbian population needed protection. Once again, British troops formed a large part of the NATO-led force that deployed to Macedonia with the original aim of extracting UN observers in Kosovo should the need arise. After an air campaign was launched against Serbia to persuade President Milosevic to evacuate Kosovo, it soon became clear that a large ground force would have to be inserted into Kosovo to prevent the return of Serbian forces and to act as peace-keepers between the warring factions.

The large numbers of British forces involved in Operation Agricola required a correspondingly large number of RLC units for support. The first logistic unit to enter Kosovo, 23 Brigade Support Squadron of 27 Transport Regiment, crossed the border along with the front line troops on 10 June. The deployment of 23 Pioneer Regiment to Kosovo marked the first deployment of Pioneers on a regimental level since the Second World War. As is the case in Bosnia, the long-term commitment of British forces to Kosovo requires a steady rotation of RLC units to provide the necessary support to British troops deployed there.

Apart from operational duties, the first years of The Royal Logistic Corps have seen events of historical significance for Britain and its armed forces in general, and for the corps in particular. There has been a large reduction in British forces in Germany and Belize, along with the withdrawal of the allied garrison in Berlin and the return of Hong Kong to China. The

At the End of the Day, painted by Johnny Jonas, 1996–97, to mark the handover of the British Crown Colony of Hong Kong to China. The painting commemorates the service given to the colony by all those members of The Royal Logistic Corps, their predecessors, supporting civilian staff and members of the Hong Kong Military Service Corps. In the colouring of the harbour and sky, the painting depicts uncertainty about the future, while activity across the harbour marks the arrival of the new and departure of the old. The central theme, however, emphasises the strength and vibrancy of Hong Kong business and the flexibility, ambition and hard work of its people. It is a painting depicting many aspects of Hong Kong and is an expression of confidence and hope for the future.

growth of Defence Agencies, containing a mixture of military and civilian employees, has continued apace. The Army Base Storage and Distribution Agency (ABSDA) and the Defence Transport and Movements Executive (DTMX) both came into existence on 5 April 1995 and represented a fundamental change in the manner in which these central functions of the RLC were to be carried out. In April 1999 these agencies acquired greater tri-service responsibilities. Other organisational changes have included the formation of Defence Munitions (DM) on 1 April 1999 and the re-titling of the Defence Postal and Courier Agency and the former Postal and Courier Depot as the British Forces Post Office.

On a lighter note, The Royal Logistic Corps made an invaluable yet little known contribution to the solar eclipse event in Britain in August 1999. ITN News had decided to film the eclipse from the Channel Island of Alderney, as the island was deemed to be the best site for viewing the phenomenon. Unfortunately, ITN's vehicles and equipment could not be transported by Alderney's light aircraft and hydrofoil ferry service, so the TV crews called upon The Royal Logistics Corps for help. One of 17 Port & Maritime Regiment's ramped craft logistic vessels, the RCL *Arromanches*, transported the ITN News team and their equipment to the island, ensuring British viewers received the best pictures of the event. Although peacetime contributions of The Royal Logistic Corps to the well-being of the nation are not always so spectacular, members of the corps frequently participate in activities, usually sports-based, on behalf of various charities.

History and tradition are vital to the *esprit de corps* of any regiment or corps of the British army, however young, and The Royal Logistic Corps is no exception. The new RLC museum was opened by HRH The Princess Royal on 13 June 1995. Costing £600,000 it was built in less than 12 months and houses a collection and archive that represent the heritage of The Royal Logistic Corps and its various forming corps. The museum staff endeavour to provide a balanced overview of the history of the predecessors of The Royal Logistic Corps, whose traditions can be traced back to the Middle Ages, as well as recording the achievements of the present. The traditions and achievements of the past are an inspiration for the logistic soldier of today and provide a solid base in an ever-changing world.

The Royal Logistic Corps has more than lived up to those traditions in its brief history and will continue to do so wherever the British army is called upon to serve in the new millennium.

THE COLLECTION

Lieutenant-Colonel J. G. Hambleton MBE

Mr F. G. O'Connell

THE COLLECTION

Hilsea Room.

The Hilsea Barracks, Portsmouth, was the home of the RAOC until the early 1950s. It is commemorated within this small dining room and in St Barbara's Church, which also contains the main windows from Hilsea Barracks Church given as a memorial to Major-General Sir Harold Parsons, Colonel Commandant RAOC. The table is the Cairo Table, used for the first meeting of the allied commanders on 22 November 1943. The inscription records the meeting and those present:

This table from RAOC Officers' Mess, Hakine House Abbassia, Egypt was used at the Allied Conference Mena House, Cairo on Nov & Dec 1943.

PRESENT:
President Roosevelt USA
The Admiral
President Inonu Turkey
Mr Winston Churchill UK
Col Warden
Marshal Chiang-Kai Shek China
Mdm Chiang-Kai Shek China
Mr Celeste
Mrs Celeste
Chiefs of Services of Allied Forces

Collections of all kinds can offer a colourful insight to the heritage and ethos of individuals, organisations, places and eras. Some are open for the enjoyment of everyone; only a few people, however, are fortunate enough to feel a close, personal association to the artefacts as they explore the displays.

The objects and works of art cared for by The Royal Logistic Corps are enriched by continuity and represent the activities of an enormous family, the members of which have served in diverse roles throughout the world. The collection has evolved through a mixture of policy, unexpected opportunities and the activities of a variety of enthusiastic individuals who have been determined to see it develop. The result, almost inevitably, is unstructured. It is essential that we find a way to understand our collection as it will continue to evolve, to be enjoyed, studied and to represent a foundation for the identity of serving officers and soldiers, as well as a wider community whose lives have been affected by our work.

One of the most significant motives for military collecting is the definition of 'home'. Serving officers and soldiers have always been subject to constant upheaval. On campaign, or simply in the course of moving from one posting to another, the ability to quickly surround oneself with a variety of familiar objects can define a tent, a trailer, a married quarter or a new mess as 'home'.

This applies as much to an individual pinning photographs of loved ones to a tent pole, as to a regiment overseas holding formal dinners in unfamiliar surroundings but enhancing the table with corps silver.

Making a strange place familiar achieves more than just comfort. A home enables one to entertain and, in part of a regiment's home, the officers' mess, this entertainment is often formal, playing an essential part in establishing a regiment within a community. It would be far too simplistic to assign the richness of a regimental or corps collection to an intention to impress official guests, but when the need arises, we are fortunate to have that means at our disposal.

Collecting to impress would, however, account for some of the earliest acquisitions. Officers originally purchased their commissions, intending not only to enjoy their military career, but also to secure friends and allies for future endeavours and to sell the commission for at least as much as they had invested. The mess – often a prospective officer's first glimpse of the regiment – had to appear attractive. Later, as soldiering became more professional, the need to attract newcomers whose academic and sporting abilities or general character would be of benefit to the regiment was just as pressing.

Once newcomers (of all ranks) have chosen to join a particular corps, their personal identity acquires a new facet. The school-leaver or graduate now becomes part

---

The table displays RCT and RAOC goblets, the ACC Horn of Plenty or Cornucopia, together with examples of maritime models reflecting the army's long-standing links with the sea and off-shore operations with military manned craft. In the background are two

Victorian decorative pieces, an ostrich and giraffe, inspired probably by the exploits of Livingstone and the colonisation of the African continent. The oil painting by Joan Wanklyn is of the Formation Parade of The Royal Logistic Corps on 5 April 1993 (see page 58).

of a large family with a fine tradition to take pride in and to uphold. Although there are formal opportunities to learn something of their new heritage, much more will be absorbed through the informal observation of displayed paintings, medals and memorial inscriptions on silver. These impressions form a small but vital part in the feeling of belonging and, eventually, justifiable pride in the achievements of one's predecessors. Early in an officer's career opportunities will arise to make a collective presentation, perhaps of a functional piece of tableware. Suitably inscribed, this piece incorporates the new member as a permanent part of the evolving story of the corps.

As members of officers' or sergeants' messes progress through their careers, many will develop a greater appreciation for history than they perhaps possessed in their earlier years. Many choose to mark their retirement or departure by endowing their mess with an inscribed piece of tableware, perhaps a clock or a painting. If the individual was involved in a significant event or operation, then he or she may wish to ensure that this particular element of history is commemorated.

Not all collecting, however, falls to individuals. Particularly significant events, or individuals whose service to a particular regiment or corps has been exceptional may be deemed worthy of recognition by the 'family' as a whole. In these cases mess or corps funds may be utilised to produce a memorial work which in quality and style is in keeping with the importance of the subject. The funds available for such a collective purchase enable messes to take on another role, that of patron of the arts. Although many officers were brought up in surroundings conducive to an appreciation of art, the fact that many regimental or corps collections contain works by leading artists is often a matter of fashion rather than appreciation, and sometimes a happy accident.

Two world wars have brought vast numbers of individuals into a regimental or corps family on a short-term basis. However brief their stay, the intensity of the times in which they wore the cap badge has led to a loyalty which can match that developed over years of service by others. Regiments and corps have therefore amassed significant collections of memorabilia from veterans who maintain only occasional contact with their regimental 'home' and regard the collection as an appropriate place for the physical evidence of their service.

The need for wider access to the collections, the presence within messes and the regiment or corps at large of a better educated and more appreciative audience, and a significant growth in the quantity and nature of material being preserved, has led to the emergence of regimental museums. Their development mirrors that of many small local museums and they have now evolved from an extended 'trophy cabinet' to centres of interpretation and education, open to all and responding to enquiries from across the world.

What then of The Royal Logistic Corps' collection, a growing, living display held and appreciated at the home of the corps who, as a family, are committed to its care and evolution? Can it be seen as a document which accurately reflects the history of the corps? No collection is ever free from the fashions and prejudices of collectors and they are all the richer for these. The museum library contains a variety of carefully written and researched histories that, between them, mark the contribution of our predecessors to the nation's history. The media and the Civil Service record the impact of today's activities on world affairs. Our historic collections, however, bring colour and character to dry and dusty words, life and eccentricity to the holders of titles and awards. Above all, they present to our newest members not only a simple account of our predecessors' achievements, but also the challenge of matching those achievements and setting new goals for our successors.

Silver Shooting Cup.

This beautifully proportioned piece of Georgian silver of 1773 was reallocated to a new use by the application of a George VI RASC badge and the inscription 'RASC Inter Unit Rifle Competition'.

Silver-gilt Tankard.

This heavily embossed silver-gilt tankard dates from 1830 and was presented to the RASC HQ Mess by the Honorary Colonels of the Divisional RASC (TA) to commemorate the 50th Anniversary of the RASC in 1968.

The Warwick Vases.

This pair of Warwick Vases was made in 1814 by Paul Storr, perhaps the most significant silversmith of the early 19th century. These wine coolers, with removable liners, were bought by the RASC officers of Bulford as a memorial to the ASC officers who passed through Bulford Camp on their way to serve in the British Expeditionary Force in France during the First World War. The term 'Warwick Vase' derives from 1770 when the Earl of Warwick visited the ruins of Hadrian's villa near Rome on his grand tour. There he heard the story that a substantial marble vase had been hidden in the middle of the lake to save it from vandals. The earl had the lake drained, the vase was recovered and is now on display in the Burrell Museum, Glasgow.

Dining Room.

This scene is from the RLC HQ Officers' Mess at Deepcut and shows the Skinner's Horse table set for dinner. James Skinner, an Anglo-Indian, raised Skinner's Horse in 1854 and the regiment fought through all the campaigns in India and beyond to the present day. After the Second World War, one of the two regiments disbanded and this table came into the hands of the HQ RASC Officers' Mess in Aldershot. It is decorated with individual goblets dating from 1893 and by the RCT Bicentenary centrepiece of 'Stacked Drums' commemorating the grant of the Royal Warrant to the Royal Waggoners on 7 March 1794. Also displayed is a pair of Mark X General Service Waggons owned by the RCT and RAOC Trustees. Beyond the dining table are three portraits by Mara McGregor of the Colonel-in-Chief, HRH The Princess Royal, and her two Deputy-Colonels-in-Chief, HRH The Duke of Gloucester and HRH The Duchess of Kent.

The Delhi Magazine.

(LEFT) Many of the 19th century military campaigns on the Indian subcontinent, both successful and otherwise, have been commemorated in paintings or by pieces of silverwork. The Delhi Magazine defence took place at the outbreak of the Indian Mutiny in 1857, when the gallant actions of Lieutenant George Forrest, Lieutenant William Raynor and Conductor John Buckley, all of the Bengal Ordnance Department, were rewarded with the Victoria Cross.

Military Train.

(RIGHT) This entrée, or chafing dish, is the earliest piece of regimental silver owned by any of the Forming Corps. It is a piece of Sheffield plate made by Elkington in 1862 and used by 7th Battalion, the Military Train. The Military Train saw service in China, Japan, India, Canada, New Zealand and Abyssinia until it was disbanded in 1869. Battle honours won during this period were Lucknow, Taku Forts and Pekin.

The West Moors Epergne.

(BELOW) This piece was purchased in the 1980s jointly by the Corporals' Mess of the RAOC Petroleum Centre and the RAOC Trust. The original piece was designed to display fruit over a mirrored base and was first presented in 1876. The inscription reads:

'Presented to Mr Edward Holden as a memento of respect on his coming of age. By the employees of his respected father, E T Holden Esq Currier. Walsall Aug 21st 1876'.

The Stag.

(ABOVE) This epergne is another example of links between the army and the livery companies of the City of London. The Stag represents the motto of the Worshipful Company of Cooks, 'Wounded but not Defeated', and was presented to the Company by its Master when his term of office ended in 1879. The piece was subsequently presented to the ACC in 1976 and by them to The RLC on its formation on 5 April 1993.

The Dalton VC Centrepiece.

The Battle of Rorke's Drift took place on 22/23 January 1879 and was perhaps the best known incident in the Zulu Wars. The Zulus, with few modern weapons but huge numerical superiority, surprised the British at Isandhlwana on 22 January 1879 and the massacre resulted in 850 British dead. The Zulus immediately moved on to Rorke's Drift which was a supply and ammunition depot only one hour away. The small contingent of 24th of Foot (later the South Wales Borderers) and various attached troops were commanded by Lieutenant Chard of the Royal Engineers and supported by Lieutenant Bromhead of the 24th Foot. The fiery confrontation between the Zulus and 144 British troops over 18 hours is one of the epic stories of late Victorian involvement on the African continent. Eleven Victoria Crosses were awarded, the most ever for a single action. The ASC and Commissariat and Transport Department personnel present were:

Assistant-Commissary W. A. Dunne – Mentioned in Despatches

Acting Assistant-Commissary J. L. Dalton –Victoria Cross

Acting Storekeeper L. A. Byrne – Mentioned in Despatches; died of wounds

Corporal F. Attwood –Distinguished Conduct Medal

The piece was commissioned by RLC units at Abingdon.

Strawberry Bowl.

(BELOW) This filigree bowl of silver plate was presented to the RASC Officers at Aldershot by Miss Evelyn Brownrigg in memory of her father, Colonel H. J. B. Brownrigg CB, Deputy-Commissary General in Aldershot 1884–86. Colonel Brownrigg's medals are in the RCT Medal Collection and are featured in this book (see page 134).

OSC Challenge Cup.

(ABOVE) This silver and gilt cup is probably the earliest trophy of the Ordnance Staff Corps. Designed with three handles as a loving cup, it was presented in 1890 to the Ordnance Staff Corps for annual competition at their regimental sports by C. Harrington. Recorded winners were:

1890	L/Cpl. W. Campbell	C Coy
1891	Pte. W. M. Rose	B Coy
1892	Pte. M. J. O'Neil	E Coy
1893	Pte. M. J. O'Neil	A Coy
1894	Pte. C. S. Penfold	4 Coy

The Spanish Cup.

This small Victorian silver cup of 1899 was presented to the officers of the ASC Aldershot by Don Mariano Belso, an officer in the 1st Regiment of the Spanish Intendency. This date again coincides with the comparatively recent opening of the new Officers' Mess in Stanhope Lines, Aldershot in 1895 where, with encouragement from fellow officers and probably after a long equitation course, Captain Don Mariano Belso was persuaded to commemorate his time among ASC friends.

The Africa Bowl.

In 1895 a new Officers' Mess was built in Aldershot for the ASC. Encouragement of the military sort was probably applied to collect new silver to commemorate the activities of the ASC over the previous 20 years. The Africa Bowl was a piece commissioned by 51 officers who had served in Africa from 1879. The inscription reads:

'This bowl was presented in 1896 to commemorate the part played in the attempted relief of General Gordon and in the Zulu War by those officers of the Commissariat Transport Staff whose names are inscribed on the base.'

One of the subscribers was Lieutenant & Riding Master Lyons, grandfather of Major-General A. W. Lyons, the latter being head of The RLC 1998-99.

The General Buller Casket.

General Sir Redvers Buller VC became the Quartermaster General of the Army some 12 years before the Boer War of 1899–1902. He was the driving force in establishing a proper structure for transport, supply and logistic support. This system enabled the British army to sustain its many and varied expeditions throughout the world, and culminated with the massive build-up of stores and ammunition needed for the First World War. This casket, in silver-gilt and enamel on a marble base, was made by Elkington of Birmingham in 1900. The inscription on the scroll reads:

'Presented to General The Right Honourable Sir Redvers Buller. A gift with the Freeman's Scroll of the Mayor, Aldermen and Burgesses of The County Borough of Southampton on his return from South Africa 10 November 1900.'

This beautiful item, together with its original scroll, was bought at auction by Brigadier John Lofts MBE on behalf of the RCT Museum in Exeter in 1988.

The Snake Bowl.

This spectacular bowl, with two applied Medusa heads embossed with cavalry and infantry battle scenes, dates from 1918 and was presented by a number of temporary officers of the corps to the RAOC Headquarters Officers' Mess in 1919. The Great War was over, the AOC and AOD had combined and, with the award of the prefix 'Royal', had become the RAOC. All those officers who had served on emergency commissions, having survived the war, were prevailed upon to make this splendid presentation to the new RAOC and its Officers' Mess. Newly commissioned officers are still called upon to donate silver, albeit of lesser stature.

The Hope Bowl.

This Georgian-style 1900 wine cooler was presented to the ASC Headquarters Officers' Mess by Colonel L. A. Hope CBE to commemorate his appointment as the first ASC aide-de-camp to King George V. This is a Monteith Bowl with a detachable upper section which could be added or removed, depending on whether glasses were to be cooled or not.

The Bacchus Claret Jug.

This claret jug, with its ornate half-goat, half-man design making such a striking lid, was the Army Cricket Cup and was presented permanently to the ASC after consecutive victories in 1907, 1908 and 1909.
Winning members of the team were:

Captain R. B. Airey	Captain C. E. Watling	Captain W. N. White
E. H. Fitzherbert	Captain H. C. F. Cumberlege	J. C. L. Godfrey
Captain L. R. Beadon	Captain H. S. Wright	G. E. Badcock
Captain A. V. Udal	SSM F. A. McLaren	

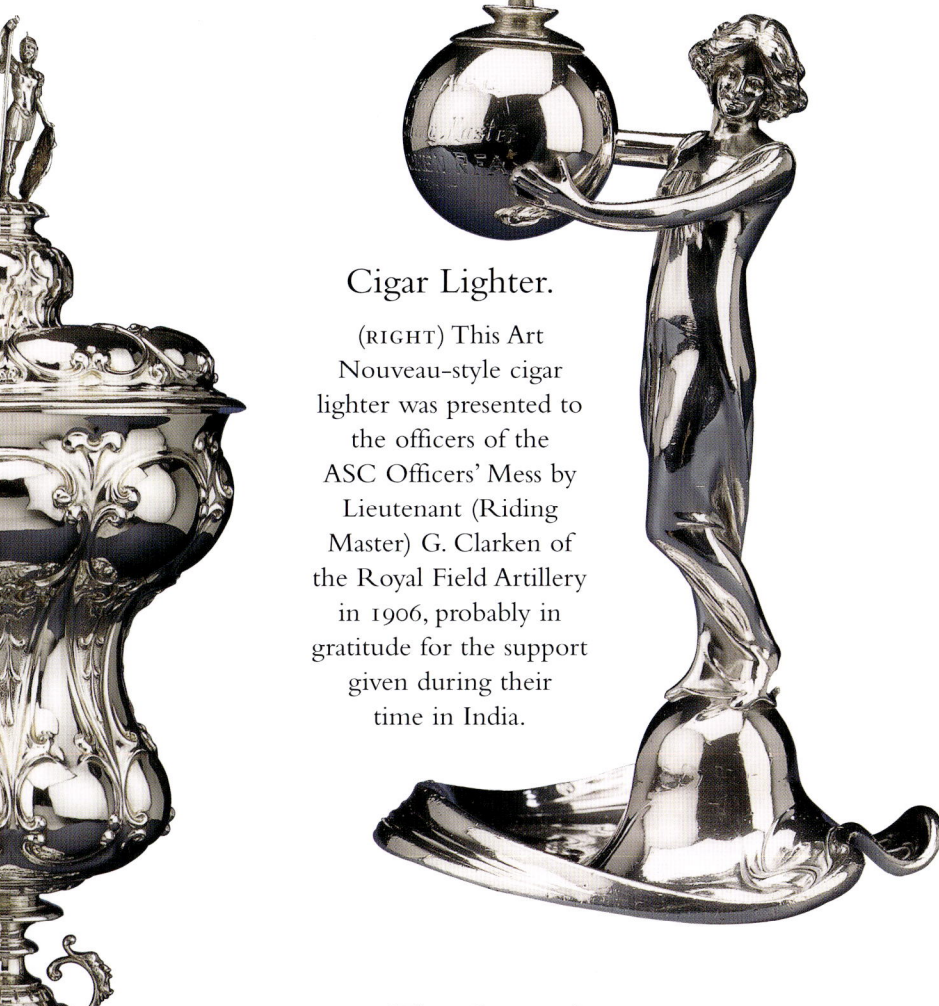

Cigar Lighter.

(RIGHT) This Art Nouveau-style cigar lighter was presented to the officers of the ASC Officers' Mess by Lieutenant (Riding Master) G. Clarken of the Royal Field Artillery in 1906, probably in gratitude for the support given during their time in India.

The Centurion.

(LEFT) Although known as the Centurion, this 1899 vase is more likely to depict one of the Roman gods. The inscription reads:

'Presented by RAOC Officers Far East Land Force to HQ RAOC Officers' Mess and subsequently re-allocated in 1961 to Eastern Command as the Inter-Athletic Challenge Cup (Minor Units) redesignated Southern Command in 1968'.

Army Football Cups.

These replica Warwick Vases were presented to the winning unit team in the Army Football Challenge Cup.
The winning teams represented are:

(LEFT) RAOC Winner of the Army Cup – RAOC SC (South) 1928

(CENTRE) RASC Winner of the Army Cup – ASC 1913–14

(RIGHT) RASC Winner of the Army Cup – RASC Training Centre 1936–37

Albion Truck.

This substantial piece from 1915 stands 24 inches high and 48 inches long and depicts one of the earliest army lorries, the Albion. Surrounding the Albion are four scenes of soldiers carrying out various functions of transport and supply. The officers of No 1 Reserve ASC MT Depot, Grove Park, London presented this piece to the Grove Park Officers' Mess in 1916. As Grove Park was the first army driver training organisation in the war, it is appropriate that this piece should should now be located in the Defence School of Transport at Leconfield in Yorkshire.

Second World War Memorial Silver.

(ABOVE) As the officers at Bulford had commemorated their fellow officers who died in the First World War, so the officers of the RASC of the Regular and Territorial Armies presented a rosebowl and two hexagonal vases to their Headquarters Mess as a tribute to the achievements of the corps in the Second World War. Hallmarked in 1919, these pieces were purchased in 1948.

Small Collection of Silver Pieces.

(RIGHT) This collection of items represents some of the hundreds of small items of silver collected over the last 110 years in various Messes.

Goblet: Presented to the RAOC by Sir Christopher Leaver CBE, Lord Mayor of London 1981–82.

Cigar Lighter: Presented by Major-General A. F. J. Elmslie CB CBE on retirement, 1960.

Trophy: South West Middlesex Football League Trophy 1944–45, Feltham.

Finger Bowl: RASC No 71 Junior Officers Course 1958. Officers included Lieutenant-Colonel J. G. Hambleton MBE, first RLC Regimental Secretary.

Ink Stand: Presented by 15th Ordnance Officers Course and 7th Young Officers Course, December 1951.

Finger Bowl: RASC No 68 Junior Officers Course 1956. Officers included Lieutenant-Colonel M. H. G. Young, editor of The RLC journal.

The Transportation & Movements Centrepiece.

The piece, with a substantial wooden base surmounted by figurines,
was commissioned by the officers past and present of the Royal Engineers
(Transportation & Movement Control) on the transfer of those functions to
the RCT on 15 July 1965. The centrepiece is held by
17 Port & Maritime Regiment in Marchwood.

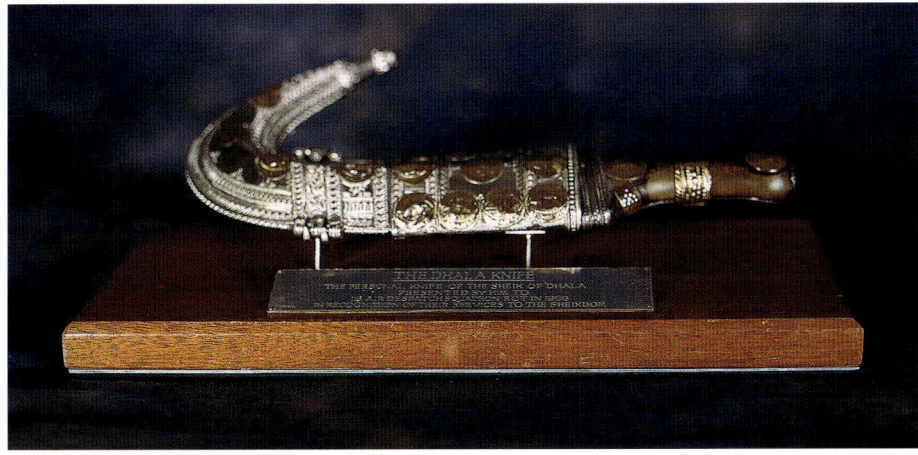

The Dhala Khanjar.

(LEFT) The personal khanjar of the Sheikh of Dhala, Aden was presented by him to 16 Air Despatch Squadron RCT in 1966 in recognition of their services to the sheikhdom. 16 Squadron has since re-roled as a tank transporter squadron and is now under the command of 7 Transport Regiment RLC in Germany.

The London District Bowl.

(BELOW LEFT) This is another fine example of an older piece of silver restored for a new purpose. This Victorian rose bowl was re-commissioned by Headquarters London District to commemorate the formation of the RCT from the RASC and other corps on 15 July 1965, changes prompted by the McLeod Committee.

RCT Truck.

(BELOW) Thought to be locally made in silver plate, this is a model of the best known 10-ton truck of the late 1960s and early 1970s. Commissioned by the officers of 4 Divisional Transport Regiment RCT in 1974, the vehicle was known to all drivers as a 'Knocker'. This centrepiece is currently located with 7 Transport Regiment RLC in Germany.

The Wheelbarrow.

The 1975 model depicts an Ammunition Technical Officer with a mechanical device named the Wheelbarrow, which searches for and destroys explosive devices by remote control. It has saved many lives since its introduction and continues to do so. The centrepiece was commissioned by the RAOC Headquarters Officers' Mess on its opening at Deepcut on 28 November 1975 by the Quartermaster-General, Lieutenant-General Sir William Jackson CBE KCB MC ADC.

Felix.

The term 'Felix' is used as a call sign by which RAOC (and now RLC) bomb disposal teams are known on the army radio network. This piece was made by Mr A. G. Sykes, Chief Designer of Garrards, based on, in his own words:

'The idea of the warrior slaying the dragon. There is an attempt to suggest the anonymity of the warrior and his loneliness. Also, I have tried to underline the ultimate moment of solitary face-to-face confrontation with a bomb – looking down the throat of the dragon.'

Anonymity was requested by some donors and the following inscription is sunk in to the base:

'This commemorative centrepiece was commissioned by the RAOC with the assistance of the following individuals and organisations.

The Royal Ulster Constabulary

Grand Metropolitan Hotels

Nobels Explosives Company Ltd

The Department of Industrial and Forensic Science, Northern Ireland

D. Seaman Esq. and R. Perrin Esq. and four other organisations who wish to be anonymous.'

Carmen Loving Cup.

(RIGHT) In comparatively recent times the army has established and maintained at private expense links with a number of livery companies in the City of London. This piece is a traditional Victorian two-handled loving cup engraved:

'This Loving Cup was presented by The Worshipful Company of Carmen to The RCT as a token of esteem and affection and to commemorate the association between these two ancient and revered bodies. Formally ratified at the Grocers Hall in the City of London on 23rd July 1975. C W LLOYD, Master, MCMLXXV.'

It was presented by the Master to Major-General W. Bate CB OBE DL, then Representative Colonel Commandant of the RCT and Major-General P. Blunt CB MBE GM, then Director General Transport & Movements, Transport Officer in Chief (Army).

Kangla Tongbi War Memorial.

The British army has a long record of service in and with the present Commonwealth countries. This Indian silver centrepiece was presented to the Director-General of Ordnance Services, Major-General M. Callan and All Ranks by Lieutenant-General G. L. Chofra, Director Ordnance Services (India) in 1978 in recognition of the friendly ties between the two corps over many years. The piece is a model of the Indian Army Ordnance Corps War Memorial at Kangla Tongbi.

The Waterloo Bowl.

This ornate bowl from 1839 depicts scenes from the battle of
Waterloo, with handles of trumpeting angels to celebrate the victory.
It was purchased to commemorate the visit of Her Majesty The Queen,
Colonel-in-Chief of the RAOC, to the corps at Donnington
on 4 June 1982.

The Berlin Victory Column.

The Berlin Victory Column or (*Siegesäule*)
was presented to Ordnance Services Berlin
in July 1987 by MAN Nutzfahrzeuge
GmbH to commemorate their long-
standing association in support of the
Berlin garrison.

The Perkins Silver.

This set is made up of silver-gilt-lined claret jugs with closing lids, together
with a gilt-lined punch bowl manufactured in 1895. They were presented by the
Perkins Group of Companies in July 1992 to commemorate the close working
relationship between the Perkins Group and the RAOC during
the Gulf War of 1991.

The Brandenburg Gate.

This piece was commissioned in 1992 to commemorate the departure of the British garrison from Berlin after the fall of the Berlin Wall in 1989. The centrepiece is silver on marble and was commissioned jointly by 62 Transport and Movement Squadron RCT, the RASC and RCT Institution and the Movement Control Warrant Officers Club. It is currently located in 29 Transport and Movement Regiment RLC at South Cerney, Wiltshire.

The Donnington High Rise Crane.

This piece was presented to the Base Ordnance Depot, Donnington in 1988 by the Norwest–Holst Dexion Joint Venture in commemoration of their joint work in the modernisation of stores handling in large military depots. It represents the high rise crane installed in Building B55.

The Globe.

The use of the globe in military silver centrepieces has traditionally implied and demonstrated 'service everywhere'. This applies especially to the Royal Pioneer Corps who, in the Second World War, expanded rapidly to become one of the largest corps in the British army, employing locally enlisted, uniformed and civilian personnel from the Commonwealth. This piece was presented to the Royal Pioneer Corps Central Officers' Mess by the former officers of the corps in 1967. It was subsequently presented to The RLC on 5 April 1993.

The RAOC Bowl.

This modern silver and gilt bowl is surrounded by RAOC soldiers and cap badges. The inscription reads:

'Presented to The RLC by the RAOC April 1993
Sua Tela Tonanti'

The motto of the RAOC translates as 'To the warrior, his arms'.

St Barbara.

This modern statuette was presented by the RAOC to The RLC on its formation in April 1993. St Barbara was the beautiful daughter of a wealthy heathen named Dioscorus who, fearing that she might marry and leave him, shut her in a tower. In her lonely existence Barbara converted to Christianity, but when her father found out, he put her on trial before the Prefect of Nicodemia, who decreed that she should be tortured and put to death by beheading. Dioscorus himself carried out the death sentence, but was struck by lightning and his body was consumed by fire.

The introduction of gunpowder to the western world in the Middle Ages (with its connotations of thunder, lightning and sudden death) saw St Barbara adopted as the patron saint of artillery and ordnance.

Victorian Post Box.

This modern working model of a Penfold Victorian Post Box was presented by Mr Peter Howard, Managing Director of Royal Mail, to the then Head of Corps, Major-General D. L. Burden CB, CBE, on 7 July 1993. It commemorates the long and lasting links between the Royal Mail and the Postal and Courier Services of the Royal Engineers and The RLC.

The Lane Memorial Trophy.

This modern silver statuette of a soldier competing in the Nordic skiing disciplines is a corps memorial to Corporal Lane of 47 Air Despatch Squadron RLC, who died in 1995. This statuette is now held by 1 General Support Regiment RLC, who have inherited the role of specialist skiing regiment in the corps.

The Grenade.

The grenade is a copy of the badge worn on the arm of all those employed in ammunition and bomb disposal within the RAOC and The RLC. This silver and gilt centrepiece was made through contacts with the Gold and Silver Wyre Drawers, the livery company with long-standing formal links with the RAOC, and now The RLC. It was commissioned in 1996 to commemorate EOD activities undertaken by 11 EOD Regiment RLC.

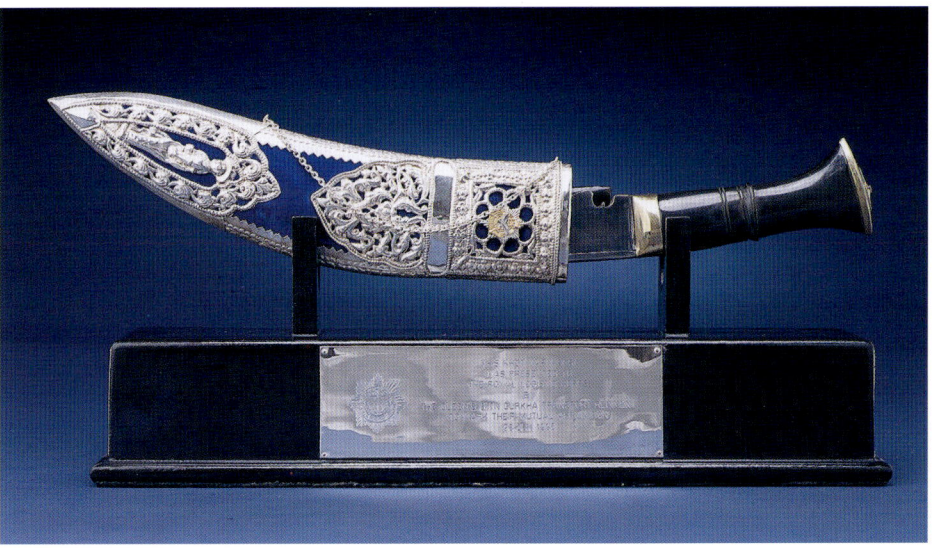

QOGTR Kukri.

This Khotimari Kukri was presented to The RLC by The Queen's Own Gurkha Transport Regiment to mark their affiliation on 26 June 1998. The kukri is a traditional knife of Gurkha soldiers from Nepal, whose courage and martial prowess are legendary. In the past they had the reputation of decapitating their enemies in battle. This knowledge contributed in no small way to the eagerness of the Argentinian conscripts to surrender rather than face an attack by the Gurkhas during the Falklands War.

Millennium Centrepiece.

The Millennium Centrepiece was made by Peter Hicks for the RLC Central Sergeants' Mess. Symbolically, it is based on the chevron shape of the sergeant's stripes and depicts the rise from Sergeant to Warrant Officer 1 (Conductor), which is an appointment peculiar to the corps and the Senior Warrant Officer appointment in the British army. They toast the Millennium.

The inscription reads:

'This centrepiece was commissioned by The RLC Regimental Association Trust as a Millennium 2000 project for The RLC Central Sergeants' Mess'.

Other silver plates list those awarded gallantry medals since the formation of the corps and some wise words on the importance and strength of the Sergeants' Mess.

FOR GALLANTRY

WO2 M. MacDonald 11.05.93 QGM
WO1 J. R. T. Balding 12.10.93 GM
WO2 A. Lane 12.10.93 QGM
WO2 R. A. Wharton 5.7.94 QGM
WO2 A. N. Joy 22.11.94 QGM
WO1 R. J. MacLelland 22.11.94 QGM
WO1 N. M. Thomsen 9.5.95 GM
WO1 A. Islam QGM 23.1.98 GM
SSGT. R. E. Brown 7.5.99 QGM

'The sergeant is the Army.'
Dwight D. Eisenhower, 1972

'The backbone of the Army is the non-commissioned man!'
Rudyard Kipling, 1896

'As a rule it is easy to find officers but, it is sometimes very hard to find non-commissioned officers.'
Napoleon, 1809

The selection of the Central Sergeants' Mess as the recipient of the corps Millennium Centrepiece is symbolic, as it is the mess into which every young soldier should aspire, and the mess from which so many excellent soldiers move on commissioning.

PAINTINGS

Game birds attributed to Pieter Casteels.

This painting has no military connection other than being purchased in the 1980s by the RAOC HQ Officers' Mess. Painted in 1684, it is attributed to Pieter Casteels, an artist well-known for country house scenes of this type. The painting is unsigned and there is a view that it could also have been painted by Marmeduke Craddock (1660–1716).

Victory under Tow at Gibraltar, by George Clarkson Stanfield.

This painting is a mock-up in oil on wood for an original unveiled in 1858. It depicts the return to Gibraltar of the body of Admiral Nelson on HMS *Victory* immediately after the battle of Trafalgar in 1805. *Victory* is towed by HMS *Euralyus*, and Nelson's body lay stored in rum to preserve it for the subsequent journey to England.

Camp of the 2nd Division.

The RLC Museum archives contain a large leather-bound, first edition book by Mr Simpson entitled *The Seat of War in the East* containing narrative and sketches of the Crimean War in 1855. Most such books have long since been broken up. This print shows the camp of the 2nd Division at Balaclava looking east. Mr Simpson's own words, written at the time of the original sketches, graphically describe the conditions during the early days of the Crimean campaign.

'The camp of the First Division can now be seen in the distance, on the far edge of the plateau, and between it and the windmill is a camp of Zouaves. This windmill was one of the most conspicuous landmarks in the position, and of inestimable value to a bewildered wanderer amongst the mazes of tents which stretched for miles away in every direction, with a provoking uniformity not unfrequently puzzling to the "oldest inhabitants" of the camps. Not the least comfortless among the numerous sufferers from the rigour of the winter in this Ishmaelitish form of existence were the wretched horses, which may be seen picketed in various directions amongst the tents, and exposed to the bitterest weather, with but scanty clothing at the best, and too often with none whatever.

There are few amongst the British public who have not visited Chobham or Aldershot, and who are not therefore familiar with the picturesque appearance presented by a canvass town on a fine day, and beneath a summer sky. A smaller number perhaps are acquainted with the peculiarly unreal and phantasmagoric aspect of tents at night before the lights are extinguished; but only those who have witnessed it can form an idea of the dreary and desolate-looking objects they become with a leaden sky above them, and the snow lying thickly around.'

HRH The Duke of Connaught by John St Helier Lander after John Singer Sargent.

In recognition of its work in South Africa, 1899–1902, the ASC was honoured by the appointment of HRH The Duke of Connaught as its Colonel. The first inscription reads:

'Field Marshal Duke of Connaught
Colonel Army Service Corps 1902–1918
Colonel Royal Army Service Corps 1918–1932
Colonel-in-Chief Royal Army Service Corps 1932–1942'

On the back of the painting is a further inscription which reads:

'HRH The Duke of Connaught
Copied from the portrait by John Singer Sargent RA
By John St Helier Lander 1913'.

Lieutenant C. G. C. Blunt by Snaffles.

The use of cartoons to make satiric social comment was particularly common in the 18th and 19th centuries. This sketch by Snaffles is of Lieutenant C. G. C. Blunt (later Brigadier) and alludes in the margins to the fact that Blunt was the only ASC officer to attend the Royal Engineers Ballooning course at Aldershot in 1906 under the guidance of the famous aviator, Colonel Sam Cody, and was an early MT enthusiast.

The Terms of the Armistice 3rd & 4th November 1918 by Herbert A. Oliver, 1919.

(On loan from the Imperial War Museum.)

This painting (RIGHT) depicts one of the many meetings between the senior officers and politicians prior to the signing of the Treaty of Versailles in 1919. Among those identifiable in the painting are:

Colonel Nagai, Leader of the Japanese Delegation

H. E. Orlando, Prime Minister of Italy

M. Venizelos, Prime Minister of Greece

Arthur Balfour, Foreign Secretary of Great Britain

Marshall F. Foch, Generalissimo, Allied Forces

General Sir H. Wilson, Chief of the Imperial General Staff

Field Marshal Sir Douglas Haig, Commander-in-Chief

M. Vesnitch, Serbian Minister in Paris

S. Pichon, Minister of Foreign Affairs for France

Mr D. Lloyd George, Prime Minister of Great Britain

Mr E. Howe, American diplomat

HRH The Duke of York.

This photograph of the Duke of York shows his first visit to Hilsea Barracks, Portsmouth, as Colonel-in-Chief of the RAOC in 1922. On the abdication of King Edward VIII in 1936, the Duke of York assumed the crown as King George VI and kept his appointment as Colonel-in-Chief.

HM The Queen by Denis Fildes, 1954.

On her accession to the throne in 1952, HM The Queen took over as Colonel-in-Chief of the RAOC from her father King George VI. The inscription reads:

'HM QUEEN ELIZABETH II
Colonel-in-Chief R.A.O.C.'

The brooches worn on the garter sash are miniatures of King George VI and of King George V, with the RAOC badge set in diamonds.

Lord Mayor's Parade 1981 by Joan Wanklyn.

Sir Christopher Leaver GBE, Lord Mayor of London in 1981–82, was a National Service officer with the RAOC.
This painting shows the Band and Guard of Honour provided by the RAOC for the Lord Mayor's Parade.
The Guard of Honour was commanded by Major K. A. Fisher RAOC.

Major-General Burden by Johnny Jonas.

The officers of the corps commission a portrait in oils of their Head of Corps. This portrait by Johnny Jonas is of Major-General D. L. Burden CB CBE, the first Director-General of The RLC. It reflects General Burden's service in Hong Kong in his choice of uniform, his love of cricket (as a member of the Marylebone Cricket Club) and the symbolic raising of the Corps flag on 5 April 1993.

Major-General White by Johnny Jonas.

A portrait of the second Director-General of the RLC was commissioned by the corps in 1997. This painting of Major-General M. S. White CB CBE portrays his service as Commander Force Maintenance Area during the Gulf War. He is wearing desert camouflage uniform and stands in front of a DROPS vehicle which was used to sustain the 1st (BR) Armoured Division.

Lord Mayor's Show by Hazel Morgan.

(RIGHT) This painting depicts the Lord Mayor's Show of November 1998 on the inauguration of Lord Levene of Portsoken as Lord Mayor of the City of London. Lord Levene has been an Honorary Colonel Commandant of The RLC since 1993. The Guard of Honour was provided by 151 (Greater London) Support Regiment RLC (Volunteers). Regular and Territorial Army Pipes and Drums were featured throughout the parade. The corps coach and various display vehicles took part in the parade to demonstrate the strong links the corps has with the City of London and its livery companies. Among the spectators were Major-General and Mrs Lyons, Major-General and Mrs Burden, and the Regimental Colonel and Mrs Gilbert.

The Mouse Cartoon by Terence Cuneo.

Terence Cuneo, well known for splendid, large paintings of military events and railway scenes, always embellished his pictures with a mouse hidden away, yet contributing to the main efforts of the event.

On occasions he could be prevailed upon to paint just mice in their own right and with their own character. This painting shows officers from The RLC and the forming corps in an imaginary Officers' Mess. The inscription reads:

'Dining In

A Mess Night in the form of a Mouse Warming party for Her Majesty's newly formed Corps (The Rodent Logistic Corps)

just returned from their first exercise on the Cheddar Flats and Caerphilly Foothills. Whilst from above the mantle shelf the portrait of their revered Rodent General, Sir Guzzlington Gruyere OGM★, gazes sternly down on the members of his beloved Corps.

★ Order of the Golden Mousetrap'

The RLC mice are modelled on Major-General D. L. Burden, Brigadier R. Bullock and Colonel C. M. Lake. Lieutenant-Colonel B. Dyson and Lieutenant-Colonel I. C. Alexander are known to have contributed to the ACC and RCT mice respectively.

Terence Cuneo by June Mendoza.

The military world has commissioned many paintings from Terence Cuneo over the years, and a dozen or so are owned by the corps and its predecessors. This unusual portrait by June Mendoza was bought by the corps from the artist in 1998 and is displayed at Mill Hill Officers' Mess, home of the British Forces Post Office, where seven Cuneos are held.

GENERAL

Oxford Painting.

This painting is unsigned and comes from the late 17th century Dutch School. It depicts the walled city of Oxford in about 1680 and shows an unusual use of perspective where the fields join the walled city, which would indicate the work of apprentices working to a Master. The silver pieces below the painting are the Berlin Bear, presented to York House Officers' Mess by the City of Berlin to commemorate the 40th Anniversary of the establishment of the Officers' Mess in 1948 based on the old Spandau Wool Exchange. This event happily coincided with the 60th birthday of the Mayor of Spandau. The other piece is a Peregrine Falcon, made by Joel Langford, with the design taken from the Coat of Arms of Surrey Heath, of which the corps has the Freedom.

Tompion Clock.

This longcase clock is by Thomas Tompion (1636–1712), clock maker to Charles II, and was originally in the Conference Room of the Board of Ordnance in the Tower of London. With its registration number of 81015051 it is thought to have been made in about 1705. It is a 30-day clock and still maintains the accuracy required of a chronometer by remaining accurate to within one minute each month.

On either side are two European armchairs donated by the RPC and a pair of paintings of a Western Nepalese Gurung couple painted by George Douglas of Darjeeling, commissioned by Captain M. H. G. Young RASC in 1963 and gifted by him to The RLC HQ Officers' Mess in 1998.

RASC/RCT Corps Church.

The Church of St Michael and St George has been the church of the ASC and its successors since HM Queen Victoria laid the foundation stone in 1892 for the Church of England Garrison Church in Aldershot. It contains many memorials to those of the corps who died in campaigns from 1882. The deaths of officers continue to be recorded on panels in the church to this day. Pictured below is the RASC/RCT side chapel within that church.

St Barbara's Church.

St Barbara's Church is an iron-clad listed building dating from 1901. By that time Deepcut was a substantial military location, having its own railway station on a spur line from Brookwood. On the closure of the RAOC elements of Hilsea Barracks, the RAOC Corps Church at Deepcut was renamed St Barbara's after their patron saint on 1 October 1967. It now contains many RAOC, and latterly RLC, stained glass windows to illustrate and commemorate long and loyal military connections over the years.

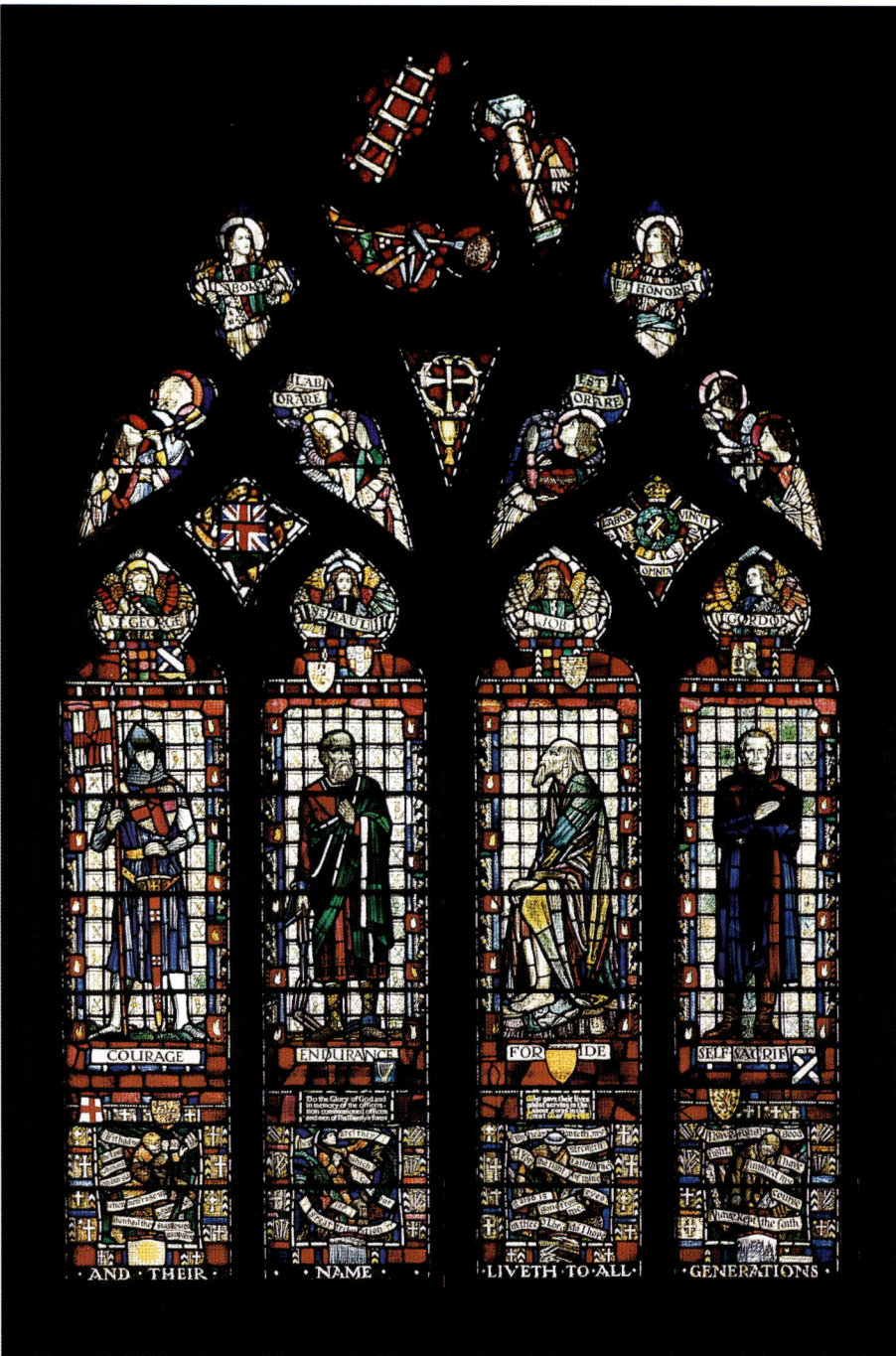

Labour Corps Memorial Window.

(LEFT) The Labour Corps Window in Blairgowrie Church in Scotland. The four main windows feature: St George for courage, St Paul for endurance, the Patriarch Job for fortitude and General Gordon for self-sacrifice. On a ruby band which separates the main figures from the lower soldier panels is the dedication of the window:

'To the Glory of God, and in
memory of the officers, non-commissioned officers
and men of His Majesty's forces who gave their lives while serving
in the Labour Corps in the Great War, 1914–18'.

The AOD & AOC South African War Memorial.

(RIGHT) Having made Deepcut their home since the early 1950s,
the RAOC and its predecessors have a number of memorials in this location.
The South African War memorial, originally in Red Barracks, Woolwich, was
modelled on Private James Barry AOC, whose medals are displayed in
the medal section of this book.

The inscription reads:

'Erected by the officers Army Ordnance Dept and Warrant Officers, NCOs
and men, Army Ordnance Corps in memory of their comrades who lost
their lives in the South African Campaign 1899–1902.'

ACC Memorial Stone.

(LEFT) This memorial stone is placed at the north end of
Queen's Avenue in Aldershot. The inscription reads:

'RAMILLIES COPSE
1941–1991

This Copse was planted to mark the 50th Anniversary of the Army Catering
Corps which was founded on this site in Ramillies Barracks on 22 March 1941.
It also serves to commemorate the service of all members of the Corps who
have sustained the army in the 50 years that followed.'

The stone was presented by the Borough of Rushmoor to mark its
association with the ACC. It was unveiled by the Worshipful Mayor of
Rushmoor, Councillor A M Ferrier, as Freeman of the Borough,
on 22nd March 1991.'

Steam Engine 'Gordon'.

(LEFT) 'Gordon' the Steam Engine is a 2-10-0 austerity engine designed during the Second World War, owned by the Ministry of Defence, and administered by the Institution of the RASC and RCT. It is now a working engine with the Severn Valley Steam Railway. Formerly, it was acquired for railway training at Longmoor, Hants, where the RE ran a military railway line from Liss, with an MOD number of AD 600.

The Corps Coaches.

(BELOW) Until 1970 when the horse transport squadron was disbanded, all officers of the RCT and its predecessors underwent equestrian training as part of their military syllabus. Later in their careers, selected officers were invited to drive the corps coaches. Two coaches dating from the mid-Victorian period have been gifted to The RLC and are privately funded to appear at the Newbury, New Forest and Windsor shows, and at Coaching Club events in London and at Royal Ascot. The corps coaches are unbeaten in recent years in the Regimental Coach Section of the Windsor Horse Show.

Warlike Stores.

Prior to the formation of the Army Ordnance Corps and the Army Ordnance Department in 1896, the Board of Ordnance provided 'warlike stores' together with a variety of other services. Their customers included both the army and navy. Pictured here are two examples of equipment they supplied. The flintlock pistol which carries a 'Tower' inspection stamp from 1844 was supplied to the Land Transport Corps and purchased by the RCT Museum with financial assistance from the Army Museums Ogilby Trust.

The 'Slasher' was designed to be fired from the guns of a sailing vessel. In flight the blades would open and tear their way through the sails of an opponent. With torn sails the opposing vessel would lose speed and manoeuvrability and its captain would be forced to choose between using his crew to replace the sails or man the guns.

Royal Waggon Train Jacket.

One of the rarest items in the care of the corps museum, this jacket, worn by an officer of the Royal Waggon Train at the time of Waterloo, was acquired through the generosity of Major H. G. Parkyn. Its delightfully intricate decoration has survived remarkably well and is one of only a few pieces of credible evidence relating to the style of uniform worn by our predecessors.

Victorian Campaigns.

A number of the objects and documents in our care survive as a testimony to the craftsmanship, care and attention to detail invested by their makers. The detailed accounts and records of campaigns, compiled in the field and later published for the benefit of others, the painstakingly drawn maps of the Crimea, and the seals and sealing wax which accompany the Ordnance Regulations date from a period when the most basic accounting could involve hours of labour. All suggest a dedication on the part of their creators to tasks which, today, would seem incredibly repetitive.

In some cases the quality of an object may reflect the affection or respect with which a comrade or commanding officer was regarded. The engraved trumpet was presented to Trumpet Major John Green by the non-commissioned officers and men of the 1st Battalion Military Train in 1863. Seven years later another officer, Captain B. Lee Warner, formerly of the Military Train, was presented with the travelling desk made by the artificers of No 8 Company, Army Service Corps.

Crimea Medals.

(RIGHT) The medals awarded to I. S. C. Morris, accountant to the Land Transport Corps are presented quite differently from the formal medal groups illustrated later in this book. Mr Morris had travelled to America after his effort in the Crimea and the medals were forwarded to his new address attached to a testimonial signed by Colonel McMurdo, the founder of the Land Transport Corps. The medals were preserved in this fashion and the complete document was presented to the corps by Mr Morris' grandson, Vice-Admiral Sir John Lea KBE, in 1986.

Tiney.

(LEFT) Tiney was a pet, probably never reaching the formal recognition of 'mascot', which accompanied 12 Company of the Commissariat and Transport Corps to the Middle East and was present at the battles of Tel-El Kebir in Egypt and Hasheen in the Sudan. Returning with his company in 1885, Tiney was killed in an accident involving a tradesman's cart. Although the skills of the taxidermist are often associated with cruel practices, we are left with a tangible reminder of a valued companion in this case. Tiney is presented wearing the Egyptian Medal and the Khedive's Star. The former was originally presented to a Royal Marine and quite how Tiney came to be wearing it we may never discover!

Military Train Shako Plates.

These plates represent the original design of headdress badge for the Military Train. Each of the seven battalions was entitled to its own distinctive centrepiece and, of the seven, six have been mounted on this card. The card and the tape which binds the plates to it were then sealed and this set would have been made available to manufacturers as the definitive pattern for all Military Train shako plates. 'Sealed Patterns' are still used as the absolute reference which manufacturers must follow in producing clothing and equipment for the armed forces. The framed pattern was purchased with the aid of a grant from the Victoria and Albert Museum.

Ordnance Clock.

This simple, but highly decorated, clock was manufactured in Franche-Comté, on the Swiss-French border some time after 1850. We are told that it was acquired by Storekeeper 1st class (later Commissary-General) Henry Gordon (brother of Gordon of Khartoum) of the Ordnance Department in the Crimea. On his return to England it served as a timekeeper in an Ordnance Depot for many years before it was presented to the RAOC Museum, still working but with an unusual sense of time.

How this clock, with its fragile decoration of thinly pressed brass, made its way to the Crimea is not known. It may have been packed with the belongings of Captain Gordon, or been a gift of our French allies. It remains with us as a rare souvenir of a campaign that was a turning point in the evolution of logistics.

South Africa.

The Boer War was a testing ground for the recently reorganised Army Service Corps and Army Ordnance Corps. The AOC provided a full range of ammunition and firearms and contrasting examples are seen here. The 64-pdr. shell is presented unpainted to highlight the soft metal studs designed to engage the rifling of an Armstrong field gun. The original fuse has been broken off, but another example is visible to the right. The Martini-Henry cartridges were discovered in an RCT museum cupboard in 1992, live and in their original packaging.

The AOC stable belt, presented to the museum by Conductor Spanner, bears the unusual 'South Africa' buckle, while the helmet is topped by the ball worn by members of mounted corps or regiments, which included the Army Service Corps. (The more warlike spike worn by others could be hazardous when working with horses.) The bust depicts General Sir Redvers Buller VC. The sculptor was W. C. Lawton, who modelled Buller's features in 1899.

Sergeant Rowland's account book is one example of an enormous variety of personal papers held by the museum – sadly he did not return from South Africa.

Creature Comforts.

A contrasting selection of supplies from the Boer War. The wine set used by General Buller is a fine example of the ingeniously packaged luxury goods which could be purchased from a variety of London suppliers and allowed the owner to maintain a standard of elegance anywhere in the world. It is in stark contrast to the bread, preserved by the RAOC museum, which formed part of the meagre rations available within the besieged town of Ladysmith.

Perhaps recognising the historic significance of the events around him, Private (later Conductor) Stupple preserved this piece of bread, which we are privileged to hold. The presentation tin of chocolate biscuits is an example of those issued to every soldier. The biscuits still retain a rich chocolate smell and the tin is accompanied by the envelope in which the recipient sent it home to his parents to keep as a souvenir – fortunately for us – but in some ways, defeating the purpose of sending it in the first place.

First World War Souvenirs.

A sombre reflection of the harsh realities of the Great War. Albert Leverett's medals, framed with the memorial plaque (or 'war penny') are one example of the huge number of such collections received in small cardboard boxes by grieving families. One man who was fortunate enough to wear his medal with pride was Driver J. F. Rawlinson, the owner of the book, *The Lost Tribes,* which he carried in his breast pocket and took the full force of the piece of shrapnel which can be seen embedded in the pages.

As in South Africa, soldiers received a presentation box, this time bearing the name of Princess Mary. In a more liberal era, soldiers received either tobacco or cigarettes, together with the pencil housed in a cartridge case. To the vast numbers of volunteers and conscripts, communication with their homes and families was essential, and the vast quantities of postcards, letters and parcels they produced and received were processed by the Royal Engineers Postal Service. The opportunity to think of home and more peaceful times was, for some, an essential escape from grim reality. It is difficult to comprehend the feelings of those who found themselves having to use such weapons as the clubs, manufactured in Ordnance workshops, in close quarter combat.

Chilwell Souvenirs.

The First World War was the first conflict involving Britain to be dominated by industrial capability. In Britain the desperate need for manpower left essential industries struggling and, for the first time, women were employed to fill the gaps left by conscripted men. These artefacts provide some idea of the dangers faced by the women who eagerly joined the workforce in shell-filling factories.

Surrounded every day by the dust and fumes of explosive compounds, the women were required to wear special protective clothing and to work with tools made of leather, copper or brass which, if dropped or banged together, would not create a spark. The vacuum cleaner seen here would have been regarded as highly primitive, but lacking an electric motor, it too was safe to use. The factories were still incredibly dangerous, however, and there was a huge explosion at Chilwell in 1917. On the day of the blast, one of the employees, who had never taken a day's sick leave and had kept her rosary beads with her at work, felt so ill that she had to return to her lodgings. This timely absence saved her life and her rosary was recovered later from the factory.

Sweetheart Brooches.

(LEFT) A small selection of brooches from the collection of 245 pieces amassed by Lieutenant-Colonel Ian Vaughan-Arbuckle, who specialised in collecting brooches devoted to the RASC and its predecessors.

Sweetheart brooches were especially popular during the First World War when people were proud to wear a visible symbol of their association with the war effort. We are fortunate to hold several examples of badges worn by essential civilian staff employed in Ordnance factories. These badges were worn not only out of pride, but also to protect the individual from abuse when seen in the street, fit and healthy but not wearing uniform.

First World War Memorabilia.

(BELOW RIGHT) Many soldiers acquired shell cases as mementoes of the conflict. This French 75mm has a carefully inscribed list of place names which record the experiences of one man among millions. The ASC officer's cap and the helmet bearing AOC markings lead us to two distinctive items of equipment. The ASC were a mounted corps and members of the horse transport trade wore the leather bandolier, less cumbersome than webbing when riding. The elegant walking stick, of which this example is the sealed pattern, conceals a sliding measure calibrated in 'hands', and was used by officers inspecting potential 'remounts' — fresh horses for army use. During the First World War any horse over 15 hands could be called to the colours if required.

Shell cases adorned many a mantelpiece after the war, often to the alarm of successive generations of RAOC and RLC ammunition specialists called to remove examples, some of which were still live. They were not very portable, however, and many, looking for a permanent souvenir, turned to the hard, slowly baked biscuits which could be issued in lieu of bread. They could only be eaten if broken up by repeated blows with the hilt of the bayonet or the butt of a rifle and soaked in liquid. Many can still be found painted in regimental colours and bearing a cap badge. This example was carved to act as a photo frame. The photograph has been lost, but the biscuit survives.

Steam.

(LEFT) The Royal Engineers were the first to experiment with steam traction in the Boer War, and in 1905 the Army Service Corps applied their experiments in practice. Steam engines were among the first vehicles in this country to be mass-produced, thus bearing a number of interchangeable components. They represented a reliable, if slow, means of pulling heavy loads, although in the field their operation could be difficult to conceal. Major T. B. Paisley presented this model, beautifully executed in paper and card. The driver's manual reminds us that, at the time, driving any form of mechanical vehicle was a specialist skill which few possessed.

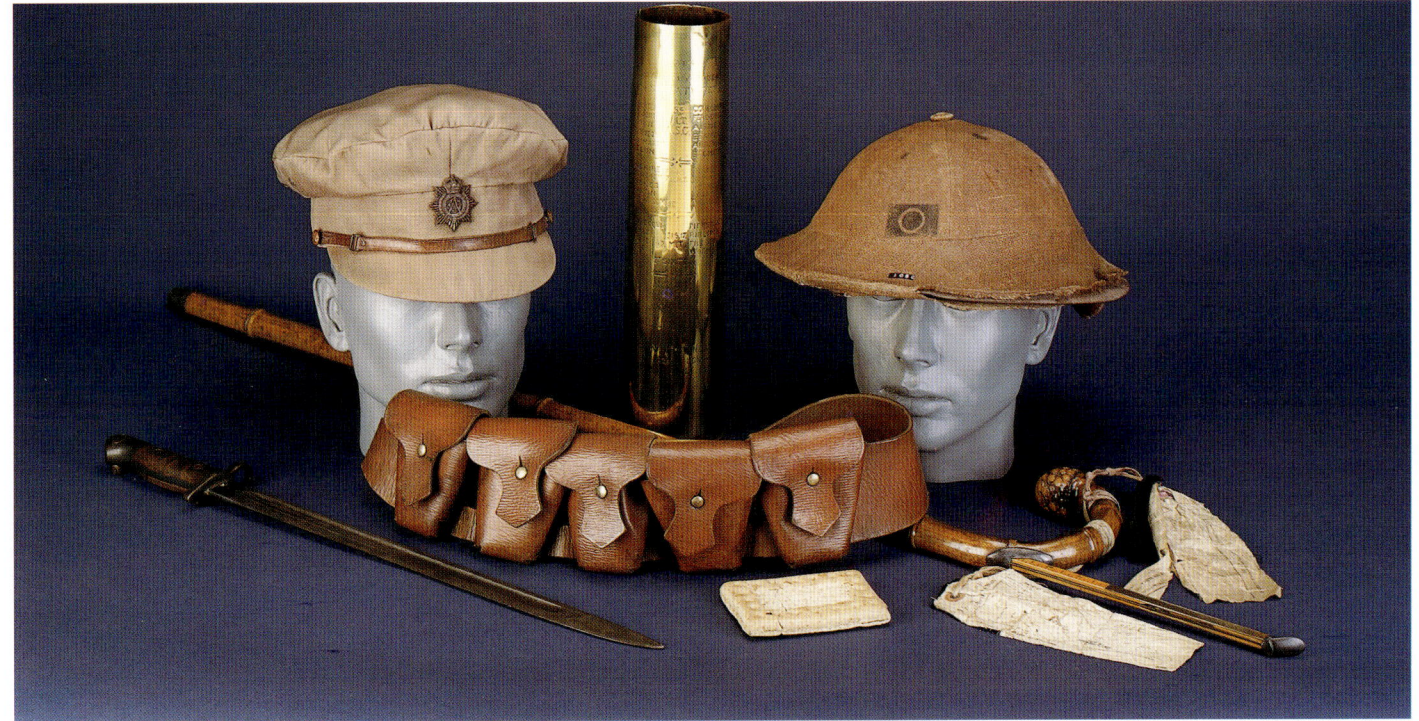

Workpiece.

After the First World War many soldiers were to spend months, if not years, recovering from wounds or illness. In spite of the care of professional and voluntary medical staff, boredom was a problem and in many cases rewarding exercise was needed to restore movement to injured fingers. This crude but incredibly detailed workpiece must have taken countless hours of care and dedication. It portrays the flags of the allied nations and a variety of observations from the Western Front. The embroiderer probably served with an ASC company supplying ammunition and it is interesting that, whilst the guns and the shells are recorded in great detail, the shattered buildings have also made a strong impression. Flanked by British and German observation balloons, a plunging Taube monoplane is symbolic of the final victory.

AOC Memorial.

The First World War had a profound impact on the whole country and communities felt the need to remember those who could not enjoy the victory celebrations. This memorial panel, which probably formed part of a set, was discovered in a partially demolished building in 1992. The artist is unknown, but it is possible to fully appreciate the loving detail which has been applied by hand to every inch of this work.

Inter-War Diversity.

(BELOW) During the inter-war years the RASC continued to provide a variety of services responding to the needs of the army across the world. This photograph, with the old Buller Barracks officers' mess in Aldershot in the background, shows through a variety of accepted dress something of the range of services provided. The two non-regulation hats, were worn in the cold of north Russia and China. The eventual seniority of the donors, Major-General Sir Reginald Kerr and Brigadier E. C. Pinden, can perhaps be seen as some form of official sanction for their use.

Technology.

(ABOVE) In spite of stringent cuts, the regular army evolved in organisation and technology. The apprentice models of the two Thornycroft lorries, a breakdown and a workshop vehicle, typify the vehicles that were developed in partnership with industry to apply the lessons of war. Overseas operations during the 1920s and 1930s, such as those in Palestine and the attachment of officers to the Sudan Defence Force, provided ready opportunities to ensure that technology evolved in England could be employed throughout the world. The finest equipment will remain unused in storage unless systems can be evolved which will allow immediate access to appropriate supplies. Ordnance officers therefore studied distribution systems in industry and at the London School of Economics. The Hollerith Card Punch Machine represents an important step in the evolution of information technology.

Chilwell.

The *Illustrated London News* was one of a number of publications which helped to preserve the morale of a nation at war. Photography and film all played their part, but the role of the artist was vital. Bryan de Grineau was an established illustrator whose work regularly appeared in its pages. In 1942 he visited the MT stores depot of the RAOC at Chilwell, a vast, highly-organised complex on the site of the First World War shell-filling factory. Several drawings made during that visit were published, but they did not include this wonderful exercise in perspective.

North Africa.

(BELOW) During the Second World War, the British army initially struck back in North Africa, tying up resources crucial to German plans.

The campaign covered thousands of miles of desert. Tanks and artillery were employed in a manner reminiscent of fleets at sea. Here, two of the most vital supplies are illustrated: ammunition – in the form of the RASC badge made entirely from shell cases collected after the fighting at Tobruk – and fuel, represented by an original example of a 'jerrycan'. They replaced the two-gallon 'flimsies', which were easily damaged and prone to leaks.

Many soldiers found that service overseas brought them face to face with other cultures for the first time. The traditional 'solar topee' or 'pith helmet' was issued to British soldiers in the 1930s and the early years of World War Two. Its design was intended to protect the wearer from a perceived danger to the brain from the rays of the sun. The more practical bush hat bears the badge of the Basuto Pioneers, who, with other companies from countries such as India, Mauritius, Cyprus, Palestine and the Seychelles, were to provide invaluable support. The Pioneer Corps coped magnificently with the need to train, employ, discipline and provide administration for men from such diverse cultures.

RASC Fleet.

(ABOVE) As war became a certainty in the late 1930s, the army quickly adopted new technology. The War Department had for decades operated a small fleet of civilian-manned coastal vessels, originally to meet the needs of the Ordnance Department. Among these were several which towed moving targets (albeit slowly) for the Royal Artillery's coastal guns. The potential genuine targets, both at sea and in the air, were liable to move a lot faster. To prepare for this, several purpose-built fast launches were ordered. This manufacturer's model of the RASCV *Marlborough* is typical. During its service with the re-named RASC Fleet, it took part in the evacuation from Dunkirk, acted as an air-sea rescue launch and engaged German aircraft in combat. Manned by civilians, it was to be the first RASC vessel to experience enemy fire.

The semaphore flags and chronometer represent the equipment with which soldiers had to become proficient. One admiral was so impressed by their skills off the Normandy beaches, that he employed RASC motor boat crews to teach small boat handling to the Royal Navy.

'Alien' Companies.

(RIGHT) In the years immediately preceding the Second World War thousands of Europeans were forced to flee from their homes. The flag is that of No. 1 Spanish Company of the Pioneers Corps, formed from a nucleus of refugees from the Spanish Civil War who were initially recruited by the Auxiliary Military Pioneer Corps serving with the British Expeditionary Force in France.

The photograph album records the activities of No 74 'Alien' Company, composed of Jewish refugees from Austria and Germany. Until the very end of the war they could only serve in Britain because of the risk to their lives and those of their families in the event of capture. The members of the 'alien' companies were often fiercely patriotic and determined to assist in returning their countries to the relative stability which they had enjoyed before Hitler came to power. Many had served with the German army in the First World War and the British media eagerly employed photographs of them with their medals.

The medals illustrated are those awarded to one of the best known members of the alien companies, Herbert Sulzbach. They are illustrated in detail later in this book.

Transportation.

(BELOW LEFT) As Britain's prosperity began to recover in the 1950s and 1960s the army was eager to embrace new technology. Increasingly, it was believed, sailors, soldiers and airmen would be replaced by advanced technology. Numerous trials and experiments to that end were conducted. Among the success stories was the 'Mighty Antar', developed by Thornycroft as a powerful tractor for use on Middle Eastern oilfields and quickly adapted for use as a highly successful tank transporter. The De Havilland (Canada) Beaver was used as a communications aircraft by the RCT and flown by pilots of the corps. The model shown here was produced by the manufacturer, and shows the aircraft with a three-bladed propeller, a configuration never used by the RCT.

Extensively tested throughout the world, but never adopted for army use, were the hovercraft of 200 and 201 Squadron RCT. Dougal, the mascot of 200 Squadron, guards the photograph here.

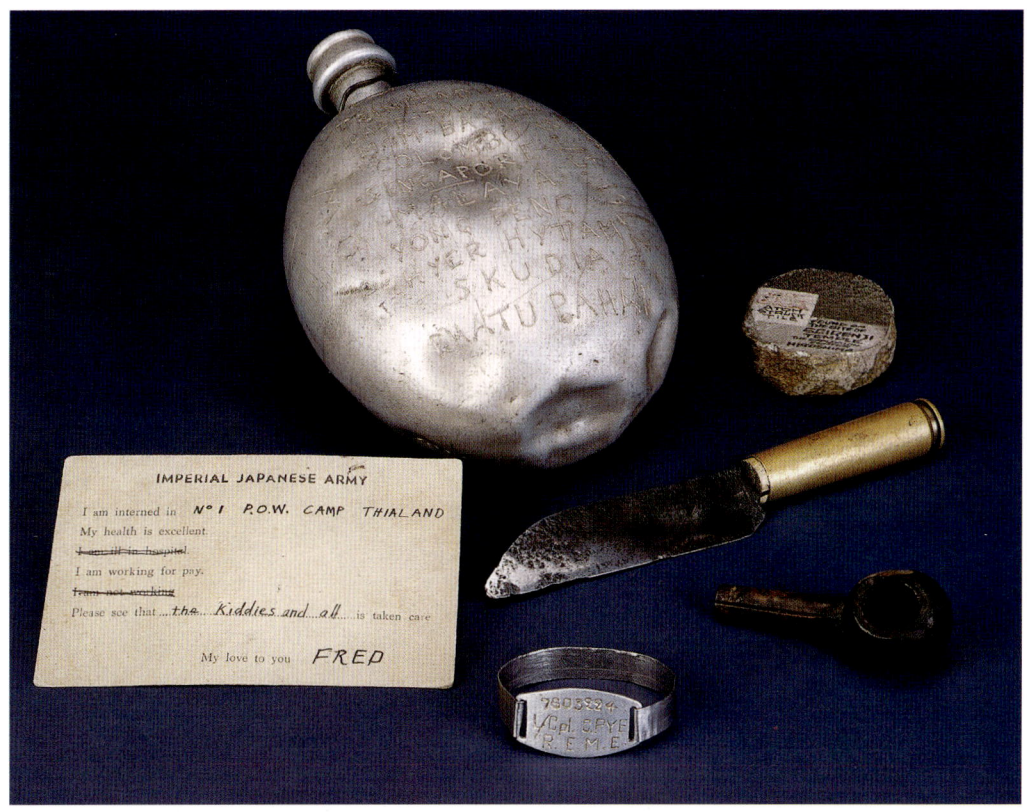

Far East.

Thousands of soldiers from the logistic services took part in the campaigns in the Far East and many were to experience the horrors of captivity in Japanese hands. The postcard was a standard form completed by Fred Pretlove. The card was completed under close supervision by his guards. The waterbottle accompanied him throughout his captivity, and scratched on it are the names of the different camps in which he was held.

Cyril Pye, of the RAOC and later REME, preserved the pipe and identity bracelet which he made for himself in a camp. At the time of his capture Cyril was a tall, strongly built man – the size of the bracelet which fitted around his wrist when compared to the standard postcard beside it gives some impression of the effects of illness and malnutrition suffered by the prisoners. Cyril survived his captivity.

After the bombing of Hiroshima and Nagasaki, it was rumoured that the guards were planning to execute the prisoners rather than surrender the camp to allied forces. The knife was one of a number of weapons, improvised in secret, with which the prisoners hoped to defend themselves against fully armed guards.

The section of tile, a curious and slightly macabre souvenir, was recovered from the site of the Serenji Temple, near 'ground zero' of the atomic blast at Hiroshima.

International Co-operation.

At the end of the 20th century the British army increasingly found itself acting at the forefront of multi-national operations.

The body armour was worn in the former Yugoslavia, as were the United Nations shoulder flashes. Later, NATO took the lead and the identity card donated by Captain Bell bears the insignia of 'SFOR' (Stabilization Force). The rest of the artefacts were collected after the 1991 Gulf conflict. Records of the inter-war period and of the Second World War campaigns in North Africa provided useful information for hastily produced publications on desert driving and health issues.

The Royal Logistic Corps.

This selection of some of the more current artefacts includes the approved design for the corps badge and cipher, executed by the College of Arms and signed by Her Majesty Queen Elizabeth II.

The hat is that worn by the first Regimental Colonel of the corps, Colonel C. M. Lake CBE, during his term of office.

The prototype of the leaflet for the new corps museum accompanies a copy of *We Sustain*, a publication reviewing the formation of the new corps. These items, however, are still focused on reminiscence or tradition; the future is represented by a prototype of a combat vest, intended to equip soldiers of the 21st century.

DECORATIONS AND MEDALS

Lieutenant-Colonel D. J. Owen MBE

The Defence of Rorke's Drift, 22nd January 1879
by Lady Elizabeth Butler.

Queen Victoria commissioned this stirring painting in which certain key individuals can be identified. Lieutenant Chard is in the centre, pointing, with Lieutenant Bromhead next to him. On Chard's left, Acting Storekeeper Byrne flings his arms in the air as a rifle bullet hits him. To Chard's right is Assistant-Commissary Dalton, his hand to his mouth, as he shouts a warning. The man firing his rifle from the window is Corporal Attwood and Commissary Dunne can be seen ushering wounded to the hospital.

DECORATIONS AND MEDALS

The highest rewards in all ages and nations have been bestowed for acts of valour and military bearing in the face of an enemy. The custom of striking medals to commemorate victories, important events, or in honour of remarkable people or deeds, dates from the times of the Greeks and Romans, but only in modern times have medals been issued as a reward for military service and worn as personal decorations. The first medal given in England for military service was struck by order of King Charles I in 1643 for the battle of Edgehill, but it was not given to all the participants. In 1650, however, the House of Commons voted that all the officers and soldiers involved in the defeat of the Scots at the battle of Dunbar should be presented with gold and silver medals respectively. This was the first medal to be awarded to both officers and men and was to be the last granted by a sovereign until Waterloo in 1815. The Waterloo Medal was another first, in that both officers and soldiers in Britain were given the same medal, as is common in today's army. A medal for the storming and capture of Seringapatam in 1799 was distributed to officers and soldiers, European and Indian, who had taken part, but this was an Indian medal.

Towards the end of the 18th century the officers of a few regiments gave medals to their men as rewards for particular acts of gallantry, distinguished service in the field, long service, good conduct and good shooting. These medals were not issued by the government, but were presented by the officers at their own expense. They were generally discontinued after the introduction by King William IV in 1830 of the Long Service and Good Conduct Medal.

Throughout the Peninsular War of 1808–14 medals were only conferred upon selected senior officers. It was not until 1848, by which time many of the veterans had died, that the Military General Service Medal, with bars for campaigns or engagements in various parts of the world between 1793 and 1814, was issued to surviving officers and men. It seems unbelievable to us today that participants of the Peninsular War and other campaigns went unrewarded for some 40 years.

In the second half of the 19th century it became customary to grant a medal to all who had taken part in a campaign. At first the awkward expedient was adopted of inscribing the name of each important battle on the reverse of the medal itself, as in the case of the Kandahar, Ghuznee and Cabul medals of 1842. When the medals were worn, it was impossible to tell which campaign the soldier had served in. This system, therefore, was far from satisfactory.

The medals for the Sutlej Campaign of 1845–46 all bore the names of the battle on the reverse and an officer or soldier who fought in any one engagement received the appropriate medal. For each subsequent battle, he received a bar inscribed with the name of the engagement.

For the Punjab Campaign of 1848–49, however, the medal without a bar was given to all men who served in the Punjab Province (i.e. those who were within the sphere of operations between certain dates). Those who had taken part in the three principal battles, Chilianwala, Mooltan and Goojerat, received bars so worded in addition to the medal. As with some more modern medals, the bars bore the dates to cover the period during which the recipients were on active service, instead of the names of the battles or places. Examples include the South African Medal for 1877–79 and the Gulf Medal of 1990–91.

General Service Medals were first introduced to prevent a multiplication of medals. In other words, the same medal was given for all small wars or expeditions in a certain country or continent or world-wide, while bars attached to the ribbon denoted the particular action for which the medal was awarded. Examples include the India General Service Medal of 1854, which had 23 different bars and was awarded until 1895; and the Africa General Service Medal of 1902 (last issued for Kenya in 1956). The General Service Medals of 1918–62 and 1962 to date, however, were awarded for operations world-wide. On 1 January 2000 the Operational Service Medal replaced the General Service Medal, which will be phased out at the end of the campaigns of Northern Ireland and Air Operations in Iraq.

The award of stars for particular expeditions and operations started in 1843, with the grant of a special star for the Gwalior Campaign. Other examples are the Kabul to Kandahar Star of 1880; the Khedive's Bronze Star for the Egyptian Campaigns of the 1880s; the Ashanti Star 1896; the 1914 and 1914–15 Stars of the First World War and the Campaign Stars for service in the Second World War.

When the United Nations (UN) was formed in 1948 British servicemen qualified for the first time for campaign medals awarded by an international body as opposed to a head of state. The first of many UN medals issued was for service in the Korean War of 1950–53. Since the end of the Cold War, Britain has been committed to a number of international operations, mainly in the Balkans, Near East and Africa, and servicemen have earned an increasing number of UN medals. In 1994 the North Atlantic Treaty Organisation (NATO) awarded its first Service Medal for Operations in the Former Yugoslavia. In both organisations the medal issued is the same for each campaign, but is awarded with a different ribbon to distinguish the area of operation or service.

Some of the medals which represent the corps' heritage have been purchased. The majority, however, have been donated or loaned by the recipients or their families. Today they are cared for by the corps museum or separate trusts, and rate among the finest collections of military medals in the country. They reflect the diverse contribution of the men and women from the forming corps and The Royal Logistic Corps who have been deployed widely throughout the world on all operations. The small selection reproduced in this book provide an invaluable record of the corps' service to the Crown and perpetuate the memory of the deeds which continue to inspire members of the corps today.

Weighing 358 ounces, the Cascabel, the metal from which all VCs are made, is all that remains of two Russian cannon captured at Sebastopol, the last great battle of the Crimean War. The Cascabel, a large knob at the rear of the cannon, held ropes which were used when the artillery piece was being manhandled. It is now cared for by The RLC.

(Medals shown on the following pages are described left to right.)

Waggoner W. Twigg

Royal Waggon Train.

Military General Service Medal
1793–1814.

William Twigg joined the
Royal Waggon Train on 2 August
1805 and served throughout
the Peninsular War until
medically discharged on
8 September 1814.

Lieutenant-Colonel T. Aird

Royal Waggon Train.

Waterloo Medal 1815.

Thomas Aird was commanding
officer of the Royal Waggon Train at
the time of the battle of Waterloo.

Lieutenant F. S. Hawkins

Commissariat Department.

Army of India Medal 1799–1826 and
First China War Medal 1840–42.

Francis Hawkins was present at the Siege of Bhurtpore
on 17–18 January 1826 and served in the First China War
of 1840–42. Although his parent regiment was the 38th Bengal
Native Infantry, he was connected throughout his service
with the Commissariat Department.

Lieutenant-Colonel T. James CB
Commissariat Department.

CB, Sutlej Medal 1845–46 and Indian Mutiny Medal 1857–58.

Thomas James was credited as 'one of the saviours of Lucknow' for his foresight in filling the swimming pool under the Residency with grain during the siege of Lucknow. Although his parent regiment was the 2nd Bengal Native Infantry, he served in the Commissariat Department and was the only Commissary officer at Lucknow during the siege. He died on Christmas Day 1874 at Calcutta, killed by a fall from his horse while pig sticking.

Major-General H. J. Brownrigg CB
Commissariat and Transport Department.

CB, Crimea Medal 1854–56, Canada General Service Medal 1866–70, South Africa Medal 1877–79 and Turkish Crimea Medal 1854–56.

Commissary-General Brownrigg joined the Commissariat in 1850 and served throughout the Crimean War, in Canada in operations against the Fenian Raid 1866, in the Zulu War of 1879 and the First Boer War in 1881, where he was Mentioned in Despatches. His daughter presented the corps with a beautiful silver strawberry bowl (see page 75).

Staff Sergeant T. Brookhouse DCM

Army Service Corps.

DCM and Ashantee Medal 1873–74.

Staff Sergeant Brookhouse's DCM, awarded for
service in Ashantee (*sic*), is the earliest won by
a member of the ASC.

Sergeant F. Attwood DCM

Army Service Corps.

DCM and South Africa Medal 1877–79.

Sergeant Attwood was one of four corps personnel at
the battle of Rorke's Drift during the Zulu War in
which Assistant-Commissary Dalton was
awarded the Victoria Cross.

Private G. R. Harratt BEM

Commissariat and Transport Corps.

BEM (Civil), Egypt 1882–89, Defence Medal 1939–45, Coronation Medal 1911 and Khedive's Star 1882–91.

Private Harratt was in the Sudan in 1884 as part of the force sent to relieve General Gordon. He left the service before 1914, became a postman and in 1937 was awarded the BEM. In the Second World War he served as an air raid warden, earning the Defence Medal, 61 years after the award of his first medal.

Private J. Barry

Army Ordnance Corps.

Sudan Medal 1896–97, Queen's South Africa Medal 1899–1901, King's South Africa
Medal 1901–02, Africa General Service Medal 1902, British War Medal 1914–20,
Long Service and Good Conduct Medal and Khedive's Sudan Medal.

Private Barry enlisted in 1895 and was in uniform for 25 years, although he
continued to serve the corps at the Royal Arsenal until his death in 1932 aged 56 years.
He is best remembered as the 'man on the top of the memorial' on the parade
square at Deepcut, a picture of which appears on page 109.

Sergeant G. W. Gordon DCM

Army Service Corps.

DCM, Queen's South Africa Medal 1899–1901 and King's South Africa Medal 1901–02.

Gordon earned an unusual gallantry award for action in Crete (Kandia) in 1898 for which no campaign medal was issued. Sergeant Gordon organised the rescue of a wounded infantry soldier when the Bashi Bazouks attacked the Supply Depot.

Warrant Officer 2 J. Burrows

Army Service Corps.

British South Africa Company Medal 1896, East and West Africa Medal 1898, Queen's South Africa Medal 1899–1901 and Long Service and Good Conduct Medal.

Company Sergeant-Major Burrows served in Rhodesia and Sierra Leone before the Boer War of 1899–1902, when he was involved in the Relief of Ladysmith. His Long Service and Good Conduct Medal was awarded during the reign of King Edward VII.

Lieutenant-Colonel A. Mullaly DSO

Supply and Transport Corps.

DSO, India General Service Medal 1895–1902, Tibet Medal 1903–04, India
General Service Medal 1908–35, Coronation Medal 1902 and Delhi Durbar
Medal 1911.

Alexander Mullaly was awarded the DSO for services with the Tibet Mission
Escort in 1904 when he served as Chief Supply Officer. He had a distinguished
career in India between 1886 and his death in 1913.

Major H. A. Rice OBE
Royal Army Service Corps.

OBE, Queen's South Africa Medal 1899–1901, 1914–15 Star,
British War Medal 1914–20, Victory Medal 1914–19 with MID,
St John Ambulance Brigade South Africa Medal and
Order of the Striped Tiger.

Major Rice commanded the Chinese Cooly Corps in the First World
War, for which he was awarded the Order of the Striped Tiger. The
St John Ambulance Medal is an official campaign medal awarded only
to St John Ambulance Volunteers in the Boer War 1899–1902.

Sergeant F. S. Betts

Army Post Office Corps and RE.

Queen's South Africa Medal 1899–1901, King's South Africa Medal 1901–02,
1914 Star and Bar, British War Medal 1914–20, Victory Medal 1914–19, Imperial Service Medal,
Meritorious Service Medal (Immediate award) and Territorial Forces
Efficiency Medal.

Sergeant Betts enlisted into the APO Corps before transferring to the RE. In January 1919
he was awarded an Immediate MSM in recognition of the valuable service rendered with the
British forces in Salonika. In 1938 he was awarded the Imperial Service Medal
for services as a head postman in the London Region.

Driver E. L. Alls
Army Service Corps.

1914 Star with Bar, British War Medal 1914–20, Victory Medal 1914–19, French General Service Medal for Morocco 1909 and French *Medaille d'Honneur* 1908.

Driver Alls served in the French Foreign Legion before the First World War and took part in French operations in Morocco, 1908–09. He was awarded the *Medaille d'Honneur* for saving life. In 1914 he was released to return to the British army for the war.

Conductor F. G. Leaney DCM
Army Ordnance Corps.

DCM, 1914 Star and Bar, British War Medal 1914–20, Victory Medal 1914–1919 with MID, Long Service and Good Conduct Medal and Meritorious Service Medal.

Conductor Leaney was awarded the DCM for conspicuous gallantry during a fire at an ammunition depot when, at great risk, he removed a number of trucks loaded with ammunition, which would have otherwise been destroyed.

Farrier Sergeant T. Cussens DCM MM

Army Service Corps.

DCM, MM, 1914 Star and Bar, British War Medal 1914–20, Victory Medal
1914–19 and Long Service and Good Conduct Medal.

Sergeant Cussens earned his DCM at Ypres on 5 November 1914 when he
rescued 147 horses from stables that were demolished by shellfire; he was
awarded the MM in 1917. He came from Farnborough and received
his DCM from King George V on Queen's Parade, Aldershot.

Lieutenant–Colonel R. Chalkley OBE GM
Royal Army Ordnance Corps.

OBE, GM, 1914–15 Star, British War Medal 1914–20, Victory
Medal 1914–19, General Service Medal 1918–62, 1939–45 Star,
Burma Star, Defence Medal 1939–45, War Medal 1939–45 and Territorial
Army Efficiency Medal (with Honourable Artillery Company ribbon).

An able seaman in the Royal Navy Volunteer Reserve in 1915, Chalkley
became a lieutenant in Iraq in the 1920s in the RA and a captain in the
RAOC in the Second World War, when he was awarded the GM for
bomb disposal work in 1940. He gained his OBE for service in Burma.

Colonel E. D. G. Galley OBE MC AFC

Royal Army Service Corps.

OBE, MC, AFC, 1914–15 Star, British War Medal 1914–20,
Victory Medal 1914–19, General Service Medal 1918–62, 1939–45 Star,
Africa Star, Italy Star, Defence Medal 1939–45, War Medal 1939–45
and Coronation Medal 1937.

Colonel Galley was one of 50 or so ASC officers seconded to the RFC
as fighter pilots during the Great War. He earned his MC in 1918 as a result
of a dogfight with German planes, and his AFC in 1919 for saving his
aircraft in hazardous circumstances. He had a long and
distinguished career during both world wars.

Warrant Officer Class 1 B. Cook MBE

Royal Army Ordnance Corps.

MBE, 1914 Star and Bar, British War Medal 1914–20, Victory Medal
1914–19 with MID, Defence Medal 1939–45, War Medal 1939–45, Silver
Jubilee Medal 1935, Coronation Medal 1937, Coronation Medal 1953,
Long Service and Good Conduct Medal GVR, Long Service and
Good Conduct Medal GVIR and Meritorious Service Medal.

RSM Cook was the first RSM of the RAOC, having transferred
from the Grenadier Guards in 1919. In 1931 he retired and joined the
King's Bodyguard, but rejoined in 1939 on the outbreak of the Second
World War. After the war he resumed his service with the King's
Bodyguard, in which he served until he retired
in 1963, aged 77 years.

Colonel T. Harris-Hunter OBE TD
Royal Army Service Corps.

OBE, British War Medal 1914–20, Victory Medal 1914–19, 1939–45 Star, France and
Germany Star, War Medal 1939–45, Silver Jubilee 1935, Coronation Medal 1937,
Coronation Medal 1953 and Territorial Decoration.

Having served in the Highland Cyclist Battalion and RHA during the First World War,
Lieutenant-Colonel Harris-Hunter commanded the 51st Highland Division Column RASC
during the Second World War and was captured in 1940. He surrendered to General
Rommel in the square at St Valery and remained a prisoner-of-war until 1945. After
demobilisation he was appointed Honorary Colonel 51st Highland Division
Column RASC until his retirement from public life in 1960.

Corporal J. Scully GC
Pioneer Corps.

GC, War Medal 1939–45 and Coronation Medal 1953.

Corporal Scully was awarded the GC for conspicuous gallantry during an air raid at Birkenhead. He was serving with 256 Company, which was engaged in rescue work on the night of 13 March 1941. He risked his life during a seven-hour operation to save the lives of two civilians.

Major N. L. T. Darewski DSO
Royal Army Ordnance Corps.

DSO, 1939–1945 Star, Africa Star, Italy Star, Defence Medal 1939–45 and War Medal 1939–45.

Major Darewski served with the Special Operations Executive in the Balkans and was the first British officer to join the patriots of north-west Italy in 1944, for which he was awarded the DSO. He was killed in action after a German attack on the partisans at Marrsaglia in November 1944 and was buried at Cartemelia.

Corporal K. Bilton DFM
Royal Army Service Corps.

DFM, 1939–45 Star, Africa Star, Italy Star and War Medal 1939–45.

Corporal Bilton was the recipient of one of only four Distinguished Flying Medals awarded to Air Despatch soldiers for gallantry in the Second World War. He was based in Italy and gained his DFM during Special Operations, dropping supplies to the partisans in Yugoslavia.

CAPTAIN HERBERT SULZBACH O.B.E.
SERVED WITH THE GERMAN ARMY 1914-1918
SERVED WITH THE BRITISH ARMY 1940-1948

Captain H. Sulzbach OBE

Pioneer Corps.

(LEFT)

Order of Merit Grand Cross Germany, *Croix de Paix de l'Europe*,
Iron Cross 1st Class, Iron Cross 2nd Class, War Medal 1914-18, OBE,
Defence Medal 1939–45 and War Medal 1939-45.

Herbert Sulzbach had the distinction of holding a commission in
the German army during the First World War and the British army
during the Second World War. Born in Frankfurt-am-Main in 1894, he served
in the Imperial German army during the First World War. In 1937 he came
to Britain where, after a brief period of internment in 1940, he enlisted
in the British army. He retired in 1948 and in 1951 joined the
West German embassy, where he worked for Anglo-German
reconciliation. He died in 1985, aged 91.

Staff Superintendent W. J. Paterek MBE

Mixed Service Organisation (MSO).

(BELOW)

MBE, Vatican *Exsuli Benede Ecclesia Merito*, Polish Cross of Merit 1st Class,
Cross of Merit 2nd Class, Army Medal 1939-45, Medal of Merit, Medal of
Union, Long Service 20 years and Long Service 10 years.

Commissioned into the Polish infantry in May 1939 and captured by
the Germans in September 1939, Paterek joined the UN Rehabilitation
and Repatriation Association, the CMLO in 1947 and the MSO in 1950,
where he remained until his death in 1988. In 1976 he received his MBE
from HM The Queen in recognition for outstanding service to
the crown. He served in Fallingbostel and Hamm, where he was
for 13 years Senior MSO Member.

Driver R. Chadband

Royal Army Service Corps.

General Service Medal 1918–62 and Naval General Service Medal 1915–62.

Driver Chadband earned the extremely rare award of the Naval General Service Medal with Yangtze 1949 Bar for an air operation. Ron Chadband was serving with 799 Air Despatch Company in Hong Kong when tasked to fly supplies to HMS *Amethyst*, which was trapped by the Chinese on the River Yangtze. The Sunderland flying boat successfully delivered its supplies before returning to Shanghai. The second mission was less successful.

Captain P. L. Handley-Greaves

Royal Engineers and Royal Corps of Transport.

General Service Medal 1962 to date, Long Service and Good Conduct Medal, Order of Setia Negra Brunei and Royal Brunei Malay Regiment General Service Medal 1965.

Peter Handley-Greaves enlisted in the RE in 1959 and transferred to the RCT on its formation in 1965. He spent almost all his 28-year career in the Maritime Service and travelled throughout the world, including a three-year secondment to the Royal Brunei Navy.

Corporal M. J. Driscoll QGM

Royal Corps of Transport.

(LEFT)

QGM and Gulf War Medal 1990–91.

While serving with 24 (Air Mobile) Field Ambulance RAMC during the Gulf War, Corporal Driscoll's convoy was caught in a minefield; an exploding mine injured a number of people and killed a medical officer. Despite a shrapnel wound to the thigh, Driscoll provided medical care for the injured. Corporal Driscoll showed uncommon bravery and was an inspiration to those around him.

Lieutenant-Colonel J. W. Chittock MBE

Army Catering Corps.

(BELOW)

MBE, 1939–45 Star, France and Germany Star, Defence Medal 1939–1945, War Medal 1939–45 with MID, Korean War Medal 1950–53, UN Korea 1950–54 and General Service Medal 1918–62.

Lieutenant Chittock enlisted in the RA in 1939, transferring to the ACC in 1945. After training he was posted to India as Staff Captain Catering in the Bombay area. He then moved to the Middle East via the Sudan before service in Korea during the war of 1950–53. Service in Cyprus was followed by a tour of duty in Germany prior to returning to the School of Cookery. He completed his service as Commander ACC at HQ Western Command.

Lieutenant-Colonel D. A. Holder MBE

Army Catering Corps.

(ABOVE)

MBE, 1939–45 Star, Africa Star, Italy Star, France and Germany Star, Defence Medal 1939–45, War Medal 1939–45 with MID, General Service Medal 1918–62, Indian Independence Medal.

Commissioned into the RASC in 1939, Holder served with 82 Company. In 1940 he was sent to the Army School of Cookery, after which he took up an appointment of Senior Messing Officer. During the Second World War he served in the Middle East and northern Europe, and in 1946 he embarked for India, where he served in Delhi as a catering instructor. Before retiring in 1958 he served in Singapore and Hong Kong.

Lieutenant-General Sir F. T. Clayton KCB KCMG

late RASC.

(RIGHT)

KCB, KCMG, Ashanti Star 1896, Queen's South Africa Medal 1899–1901, 1914 Star and Bar, British War Medal 1914–20, Victory Medal 1914–19 with MID, Coronation Medal 1911, Legion of Merit France, Order of Sacred Treasure Japan, Order of Leopold Belgium.

Commissioned into the Royal Warwickshire Regiment in 1876, Clayton joined the Commissariat and Transport Staff in 1882 and the ASC in 1889. During the First World War he was initially Director of Supplies to the British Expeditionary Force in France until he was appointed in 1915 as the Inspector-General of Communications on the Western Front. He was the first logistic corps officer to be promoted to the rank of lieutenant-general.

LtGen Sir H.M. GALE. KBE. CB. CVO. MC. (late RASC)

Lieutenant-General Sir H. M. Gale
KBE CB CVO MC
late RASC.
(LEFT)

KBE, CB, CVO, MC, 1914 Star, British War Medal 1914–20, Victory Medal 1914–19 with MID, 1939–45 Star, Africa Star, Italy Star, France and Germany Star, Defence Medal 1939–45, War Medal 1939–45, Coronation Medal 1937, Coronation Medal 1953, Medal of *La Solidaridad Panama*, *Legion d'Honneur* France, Distinguished Service Medal USA, Order of Ouissam Alaouite Morocco and Legion of Merit USA.

Lieutenant-General Sir Humphrey Gale served as Chief Administrative Officer, Supreme Headquarters Allied Expeditionary Force Europe under General Eisenhower during the Second World War.

Lieutenant-Colonel J. G. O. Lowe MBE
The Royal Logistic Corps.

MBE, General Service Medal 1962 to date, South Atlantic Medal 1982 with Rosette and MID, Gulf War Medal 1990–91 and NATO Medal (Kosovo) 1999.

Commissioned in 1977, Jonathan Lowe served on operations as a troop commander in Northern Ireland and in 1982 in the South Atlantic, as a squadron commander in the Gulf War of 1990–91, and as Commanding Officer 23 Pioneer Regiment RLC in Kosovo with NATO in 1999.

Staff Sergeant P. C. Twaite

The Royal Logistic Corps.

(LEFT)

General Service Medal 1962 to date, UN Medal (Bosnia) 1993, NATO Medal (Former Yugoslavia) 1994, NATO Medal (Kosovo) 1999, Accumulated Campaign Service Medal and Long Service and Good Conduct Medal.

Staff Sergeant Twaite joined as a Junior Leader in 1982. He served on operations in Northern Ireland, with the UN and NATO in Bosnia, and in Kosovo with NATO. In addition he had tours of duty in Germany and the Falklands and deployed on exercises to Poland, Denmark, Canada, the USA and Kuwait. His service clearly illustrates the life of a modern RLC soldier.

Explosive Ordnance Disposal (EOD) Gallantry Awards. Represented by the George Cross and George Medal.

(RIGHT)

The GC was awarded to Warrant Officer 1 B. Johnson RAOC in 1990 for outstanding and exemplary courage. He deliberately placed himself in grave personal danger when defusing a terrorist device in Northern Ireland to reduce the risk of injury or death to others. He was also awarded the General Service Medal 1962 to date and Long Service and Good Conduct Medal.

The GM was won by Captain T. W. Downing RAOC who showed conspicuous courage while serving in Belfast, Northern Ireland. He helped avoid a major disaster during an ammunition accident on the SS *Craster* in Belfast Lough in June 1943. He also gained the 1939–45 Star, Defence Medal 1939–45, War Medal 1939–45, MID and Long Service and Good Conduct Medal.

EXPLOSIVE ORDNANCE DISPOSAL (EOD) GALLANTRY AWARDS.
REPRESENTED BY THE GEORGE CROSS AND GEORGE MEDAL.

Awards made to officers and men of the RAOC and The RLC while engaged on Explosive Ordnance Disposal duties between 1940 and 2000 include:
GC 6, OBE 21, MBE (Gallantry) 10, MBE 39, GM 67, QGM 73, BEM (Gallantry) 20, BEM 7, MID 113 and QCB 14.

GEORGE CROSS

Jephson-Jones, R. L.	Capt.	RAOC	1941	Malta
Eastman, W. M.	Lt.	RAOC	1940	Malta
Briggs, K. A.	T/Maj.	RAOC	1946	UK – Savernake
Rogerson, S. G.	A/SSgt.	RAOC	1946	UK – Savernake
Styles, S. G.	Maj.	RAOC	1972	Northern Ireland – Belfast
Johnson, B.	WOI	RAOC	1990	Northern Ireland – Londonderry

GEORGE MEDAL

Martin, D. A. S.	T/Capt.	RAOC	1940	Gibraltar
Chalkley, R. OBE	T/Capt.	RAOC	1940	
Platel, F. V.	A/Capt.	RAOC	1941	Egypt – Masara
Telford, L.	A/SSgt.	RAOC	1941	Egypt – Masara
Thorner, E. P.	SSgt.	RAOC	1941	Egypt – Masara
Downing, T. W.	T/Capt.	RAOC	1943	Northern Ireland – Belfast
Beaton, R. W. H.	T/Maj.	RAOC	1944	Italy – Bitonto
Whittles, W.	T/Maj.	RAOC	1944	Italy – Bitonto
Pearce, F. W.	Sgt.	RAOC	1944	UK – Bradgate
McGowan, J. S.	Sgt.	RAOC	1944	France – La Brache
Pepper, G. C. G.	Maj.	RAOC	1944	France – La Brache
Smith, M. F.	T/Capt.	RAOC	1946	Germany – Emden
Kay, D. A.	Sgt.	RAOC	1946	UK – Savernake
Robson, E. R.	A/WOI	RAOC	1947	Burma – Zyatywye
Nash, K. W.	A/Sgt.	RAOC	1948	UK – Saxelby
Harley, R. V.	Capt.	RAOC	1951	UK – Hamstead
Taylor, A. T.	Sgt.	RAOC	1957	Cyprus – Famagusta
Prosser, G.	Capt.	RAOC	1957	Northern Ireland – Belfast
Proudlock, J. T.	A/Sgt.	RAOC	1957	Cyprus – Nicosia
Giblett, F. G.	SSgt.	RAOC	1959	Cyprus – Larnaca
Harrison, W. C. MBE	Maj.	RAOC	1959	Cyprus – Nicosia
Musson, W.	Maj.	RAOC	1964	UK – Aldershot
Brazier, S.	WOI	RAOC	1964	UK – Aldershot
Easterby, P. S. MBE	Maj.	RAOC	1965	Cyprus – Nicosia
Judge, T. A. L.	Capt.	RAOC	1965	Malaya – Malacca
Smith, C. W.	Maj.	RAOC	1966	West Germany – Minden

Istead, P. W. E. CB CBE	Capt.	RAOC	1966	West Germany – Minden
Hall, M. D. OBE	Capt.	RAOC	1966	Malaya Malacca
Reid, B. J. C.	WO2	RAOC	1966	Malaya Malacca
Elliott, J. F.	Maj.	RAOC	1966	Aden
Brownlee, G. C.	Maj.	RAOC	1968	Aden
Clouter, A. I.	Capt.	RAOC	1972	Northern Ireland – Lisburn
Green, T. J.	WO2	RAOC	1972	Northern Ireland – Belfast
Markham, D.	Capt.	RAOC	1972	Northern Ireland – Belfast
Mendham, R. F.	Capt.	RAOC	1972	Northern Ireland – Belfast
Dedman, A. E.	Sgt.	RAOC	1972	Northern Ireland – Belfast
Dandy, P. H.	WO2	RAOC	1973	Northern Ireland – Belfast
Mitchell, B. J.	WO2	RAOC	1973	Northern Ireland – Londonderry
Coldrick, J. M. MBE	WO2	RAOC	1973	Northern Ireland – Lurgan
McCormack, H. D.	Capt.	RAOC	1973	Northern Ireland – Belfast
Stacey, M. F.	Capt.	RAOC	1973	Northern Ireland – Lisburn
Tennant, C. B.	WO2	RAOC	1973	Northern Ireland – Belfast
Gurney, P. E. S. GM MBE[1]	WOI	RAOC	1973	Northern Ireland – Belfast
Callaghan, K. QGM	Sgt.	RAOC	1973	Northern Ireland – Lurgan
Eldred, F. H.	WOI	RAOC	1973	Northern Ireland – Belfast
Gunson, J. N. MBE	Capt.	RAOC	1973	Northern Ireland – Belfast
Newcombe, M. W.	Maj.	RAOC	1973	Northern Ireland – Lisburn
Field, C.	Capt.	RAOC	1973	Northern Ireland – Belfast
MacKenzie-Orr, M. H. OBE	Lt. Col.	RAOC	1974	Northern Ireland – Lisburn
Glasby, A. V. OBE	SSgt.	RAOC	1974	Northern Ireland – Lisburn
Griffin, A. G.	SSgt.	RAOC	1974	Northern Ireland – Londonderry
Jackson, J. A. MBE	Maj.	RAOC	1974	Northern Ireland – Lisburn
Oldham, D.	WO2	RAOC	1974	Northern Ireland – Lurgan
Gaff, J. M.	Lt. Col.	RAOC	1975	Northern Ireland – Lisburn
Bruce, R. V.	SSgt.	RAOC	1977	Northern Ireland – Lurgan
Adams, K. F. A.	WO2	RAOC	1977	Northern Ireland – Omagh
Goodrum, G.	SSgt.	RAOC	1978	Northern Ireland – Lurgan
Anderson, J. A.	A/SSgt.	RAOC	1980	Northern Ireland – Omagh
Davison, M. J. MBE [2]	Maj.	RAOC	1986	Northern Ireland – Lisburn
Hurry, P. M.	WO2	RAOC	1988	Northern Ireland – Lisburn
Knox, M. G.	WO2	RAOC	1989	Northern Ireland – Bessbrook
Mollison, K.	Capt.	RAOC	1991	Northern Ireland – Belfast
Blatherwick, M. MBE	Maj.	RAOC	1991	Northern Ireland – Lisburn
Duffy, D. A. BEM	WO2	RAOC	1992	Northern Ireland – Belfast
Balding, J. R. T.	WOI	RLC	1993	Northern Ireland – Bessbrook
Thomsen, N. B.	WOI	RLC	1995	Northern Ireland – Lisburn
Islam, A. QGM	WO2	RLC	1998	UK – Birmingham

[1 Bar to GM and MBE for Gallantry
2 MBE for Gallantry]

PRIVATE (FARRIER) MICHAEL MURPHY,
2nd BATTALION MILITARY TRAIN

PRIVATE SAMUEL MORLEY
2nd BATTALION MILITARY TRAIN

· Pte (FARRIER) M. MURPHY, VC. 2 BN MIL TRAIN ·

· Pte S. MORLEY, VC. 2 BN MIL TRAIN ·

ACTING ASSISTANT COMMISSARY
JAMES LANGLEY DALTON
COMMISSARIAT AND TRANSPORT DEPARTMENT

PRIVATE R. G. MASTERS, ASC.
ATTACHED 141 FIELD AMBULANCE RAMC.

TEMPORARY SECOND LIEUTENANT ALFRED CECIL HERRING
ARMY SERVICE CORPS

ATTACHED 6TH (SERVICE) BATTALION NORTHAMPTONSHIRE REGIMENT

· Acting Asst Comy J.L. DALTON, VC. COMT DEPT ·

· Pte R.G. MASTERS, VC. ASC ·

· 2/Lt A.C. HERRING, VC. ASC ·

DRIVER JOSEPH HUGHES, RASC.

307 COMPANY RASC.

Victoria Crosses and George Crosses of the RASC and predecessors

Farrier M. Murphy VC
Military Train, Indian Mutiny 1858.

Private S. Morley VC
Military Train, Indian Mutiny 1858.

Assistant-Commissary J. L. Dalton VC
Commissariat and Transport Department,
Rorke's Drift 1879.

Private R. G. Masters VC
Army Service Corps, France 1918.

Second Lieutenant A. C. Herring VC
Army Service Corps, attached
6th Battalion Northampton Regiment,
France 1918.

Second Lieutenant G. Rackham GC
Army Service Corps, converted from
Albert Medal to GC, France 1918.

Private W. Cleall GC
Army Service Corps – converted from
Albert Medal to GC, Cardiff 1919.

Driver J. Hughes GC
Royal Army Service Corps,
Hong Kong 1946.

EPILOGUE

Our heritage is a living spirit, represented and recorded by the collections, created and enjoyed by the corps family and our friends.

The Royal Logistic Corps comprises some 28,000 Regular and Reserve members. We are today's generation who, living and working amidst memories of our predecessors and their achievements throughout the world, ensure that our heritage continues to evolve.

Older members have enjoyed successful careers and enjoy opportunities to share memories with their comrades; others are at the beginning of their service and are joined every week by new recruits. Their skills and pride represent a firm foundation for the corps in the 21st century.

During two world wars, one soldier in every ten served with our predecessors. We are proud to be able to care for their memories and the memories of families who lost loved ones. We will ensure that those memories are sustained.

A gathering of In-Pensioners of the Royal Hospital, Chelsea, all of whom have served with one of the forming corps, photographed at a lunch hosted by the Central Sergeants' Mess in Deepcut in 1999 in the presence of military and civilian staff.

The Wreath
From the RE – RCT

The Shield
From the Royal Army
Ordnance Corps

The Star
From the Royal Corps of Transport

The Axes
From the Royal Pioneer Corps

The Motto
From the Army Catering Corps

ORIGINS OF THE ROYAL LOGISTIC CORPS BADGE

Elements of the badge reflect those of our predecessors which amalgamated in 1993.

The laurel wreath is from the Royal Engineers (Postal and Courier Services).

The outer eight point star is from the Royal Corps of Transport.

The inner shield with three cannon and cannon balls is from the Royal Army Ordnance Corps.

The crossed axes come from the Royal Pioneer Corps.

The motto is contributed by the Army Catering Corps.

The whole is surmounted by a Queen's crown to indicate a royal regiment or corps.

The Garter and motto 'Honi soit qui mal y pense' (Evil be to him who evil thinks), used by a number of regiments and corps having royal connections, was a feature of the badges of the RE, RCT and RAOC.

The RLC badge was designed and approved by the College of Arms on 12 November 1992.

In heraldic terms the badge of The RLC is:

'On a Star of eight greater and forty lesser points in Gold a Laurel Wreath of Silver surmounted by two Axes in Saltire also a Gold superimposed thereon a rounded Gules encircled by the Garter ensigned by the Royal Crown both proper and charged with Shield of Arms being that of the Board of Ordnance (Azure three field pieces in pale Or on a chief Argent three cannon balls Sable) in base inscribed Sable of Gold the Motto: WE SUSTAIN.'

SUBSCRIPTION LIST

Her Royal Highness The Princess Royal
His Royal Highness The Duke of Gloucester
Her Royal Highness The Duchess of Kent
The Royal Logistic Corps
Institution of the Royal Army Service Corps and Royal Corps of Transport
The Royal Army Ordnance Corps Charitable Trust
Royal Pioneer Corps Association
Army Catering Corps Association
Royal Engineers Association
Worshipful Company of Cooks
Worshipful Company of Gold and Silver Wyre Drawers
Worshipful Company of Carmen
Worshipful Company of Launderers

1 General Support Regiment RLC
5 Training Regiment RLC
7 Transport Regiment RLC
8 Transport Regiment RLC
10 Transport Regiment RLC – Officers' Mess
11 Explosive Ordnance Disposal Regiment RLC
17 Port and Maritime Regiment RLC - The Officers
27 Transport Regiment RLC
29 Regiment RLC – Officers' Mess
Ace Mobile Force Combat Service Support Battalion
Headquarters Bicester Garrison and 16 Regiment RLC – Officers' Mess
Cyprus Logistic Unit – The Officers
74 Headquarters Squadron RLC
St Omer Squadron RLC
150 (Northumbrian) Transport Regiment RLC(V)
151 (Greater London) Logistic Support Regiment RLC(V)
152 (Ulster) Ambulance Regiment RLC – Officers' Mess
156 (North West) Transport Regiment RLC(V)
157 (Wales and Midland) Logistic Support Regiment RLC(V)
158 (Royal Anglian) Transport Regiment RLC(V)
Catering Support Regiment RLC
202 (Ipswich) Transport Squadron RLC(V)
203 (Loughborough) Transport Squadron RLC(V)

RASC and RCT Association
Coventry Branch RASC and RCT Association
905 (Sub) Branch RASC and RCT Association
Normandy Veterans Association

Name	Rank	Initials	Honours/Corps
Adams	Lieutenant-Colonel	A. R. M.	MBE JP
Aickin	Lieutenant-Colonel	R. M.	TD
Aindow	Lieutenant-Colonel	P. J.	MBE TD RLC(V)
Allan	Major	D. L.	MBE RA
Allen	Colonel	W. E. J.	
Bailie	Lieutenant-Colonel	J. A.	Late RCT
Banks	Lieutenant	K.	
Barnett	Colonel	A. F.	OBE
Bassington	Lieutenant	J. D.	RLC
Bate	Major-General	W.	CB CBE DL Late RASC
Baxter	Colonel	J.	CBE TD
Beaumont	Lieutenant	K. D. N.	
Bennett	Lieutenant-Colonel	I. H. W.	Late RCT
Blackburn	Brigadier	S. D.	Late RCT
Bloomfield	Lieutenant	P.	Late RASC
Boxhall	Major	C. E. S.	RLC
Boyle	Staff Sergeant	T.	Late RAOC/ RLC
Bridgstock	Brigadier	P. H.	Late RASC/ RCT
Brinley	Major	J. R.	TD, late RASC
Brodie	Lance-Corporal	J.	Late RASC/ RCT
Brown	Brigadier	T. McG.	OBE
Brown	Major	J. M.	RLC
Bugler	Colonel	R. W.	Late RLC
Bullock	Brigadier	R. M.	CBE
Bunkle	Captain	O. G.	RLC
Burden	Major-General	D. L.	CB CBE
Burr	Major (Quartermaster)	P.	
Bush	Captain	R. M.	
Byrne	Lieutenant-Colonel	T. C.	MBE RLC
Campbell	Captain	W.	Late RASC
Campbell	Major	J. S.	RLC
Cann	Captain	D. R.	Late RCT
Capstick	Driver	G.	Late RASC
Carlisle	Lieutenant-Colonel	W. M.	RLC
Carpenter	Major-General	V. H. J.	CB MBE, late RASC
Cary	Lieutenant-Colonel	G D	
Cash	Brigadier	B. J.	Late RE
Chaganis	Colonel	P.	OBE
Clegg	Captain	C. J.	RLC
Coan	Major	C. W. P.	Late RCT
Cockbill	Major	P. J.	TD
Cody	Sergeant	P. D.	Late RCT
Collins	Lieutenant-Colonel	D. J.	RLC
Conlan	Major	P. D.	RLC
Constant	Mr	R.	
Cooke	Captain	G.	RLC
Cooley	Lieutenant-Colonel	R. K.	Late RASC/ RCT
Cooper	Lieutenant-Colonel	S. R.	RLC
Coppin	Major	T. M.	RLC
Couser	Major	P. R.	RLC
Cowling	Lieutenant-Colonel	A. P.	RLC
Cranwell -Child	Captain	S. A.	General List
Crichton	Mr	E. M.	Late ACC
Crockford	Major	K. H.	MC, late Infantry/ RASC /RCT
Cross	Brigadier	T.	CBE
Dalby -Welsh	Brigadier	T.	ADC
Daniel	Corporal	M.	
Danton -Rees	Lieutenant-Colonel	T. A.	Late RCT
Davey	Captain	G. W.	RLC
Davidson	Captain	K. M.	TD
Dean	Major	P. R.	RLC

Surname	Rank	Initials	Notes
Deane	Major	J.	
Dinnin	Major	R.N.	Late RAOC/DLI
Docwra	Sergeant	M.C.	RLC
Doherty	Lieutenant-Colonel	D.B.	RLC
Draisey	Major	J.S.	TD, late RCT
Duffell	Major	C.G.	TD
Edwards	Major	D.H.W.	Late RASC/RCT
Elderton	Brigadier	C.R.	OBE
Ellis	Major	E.E.	Late RCT
Ells	Lieutenant-Colonel	D.R.	OBE, late RAOC
Evans	Brigadier	A.F.R.	MBE
Ewer	Major-General	G.A.	CB CBE, late RCT
Fahey	Captain	A.P.	
Ferguson	Major	J.K.	TD, late RCT
Field	Major	J.A.	MBE RLC
Fleming	Major (Quartermaster)	P.J.	Late RPC/RLC
Flynn	Captain	M.D.	RLC(V)
Ford	Sergeant	G.A.W.	Buller Boys
Ford	Major (Quartermaster)	E.A.	Late RCT(V)
Frere	Lieutenant-Colonel	J.S.B.	MBE
Furness-Gibbon	Lieutenant-Colonel	D.N.	OBE
Gage	Lance-Corporal	R.F.	RLC
Gilbert	Colonel	N.E.L.	
Gill	Staff Sergeant	D.W.	
Glossop	Major	D.J.	Late RCT
Golder	Mr	G.	Worshipful Company of Carmen
Govan	Lieutenant-Colonel	S.	RLC
Graham	Warrant Officer 2	R.M.	BEM, late RAOC
Greenwood	Staff Sergeant	N.J.	
Grevatte-Ball	Lieutenant-Colonel	R.F.	Late RCT
Grieveson	Major	M.W.	MBE QGM RLC
Haigh	Major	C.	RLC
Hambleton	Lieutenant-Colonel	J.G.	MBE
Hammersley	Sergeant	R.	
Harmer	Brigadier	R.G.	Late RCT
Harris	Colonel	R.N.	Late RCT
Harris	Lieutenant-Colonel	C.D.M.	RLC
Henderson	Warrant Officer 1 (Conductor)	W.J.	Late RASC/RAOC
Hepworth	Major	P.	RLC
Hill	Warrant Officer 1	D.V.	Late RCT TA
Hill	Lieutenant-Colonel	O.P.	ERD TD, late RCT
Hoare	Major	R.	
Holt	Lieutenant-Colonel	G.	
Holze	Mrs	R.	
Hope-Smith	Captain	V.L.	RLC
House	Lieutenant-Colonel	R.W.E.	OBE TD
Howard	Major	W.M.L.	MBE, late RAOC
Hoy	Major	R.J.	
Hyde	Lieutenant-Colonel	M.P.	TD RLC(V)
Irvine	Lieutenant-Colonel	W.D.	
Jackson	Second Lieutenant	A.G.	RLC
Jesson	The Reverend	A.J.	CF(V)/RCT(V)
Jewell	Major	W.K.	Late RCT
Kane	Colonel	J.M.	OBE, late RLC
Kay	Captain	T.J.	RLC
Kent	Colonel	D.J.	
Keoghane	Major	S.R.	RAMC(V)
Kerr	Staff Sergeant	T.	Late RASC/RCT
Kirkbride	Lieutenant-Colonel	P.L.	RLC
Knapper	Mr	E.M.	
Krawiec	Major	P.E.	US Army
Lake	Colonel	M.	CBE, late RLC
Lambert	Captain	M.	TD, late RAOC
Lane	Mr	S.G.	
Law	Private	M.J.	Late RASC
Lee	Lieutenant-Colonel	J.A.	
Lees	Lieutenant-Colonel	T.	TD RLC(V)
Levene	Lord Levene of Portsoken		KBE
Lill	Major	T.R.	MBE, late RAOC/RLC
Lilley	Lieutenant-Colonel	M.R.	MBE RLC
Locke	Brigadier	D.N.	OBE, late RASC/RCT
Longmoor	Major	R.D.	Late RAOC
Lyons	Major-General	A.W.	CBE
Maginniss	Lieutenant-Colonel	C.H.	RLC
Manual	Major	H.	Late RCT
Marley	Colonel	A.J.	
Martin	Lieutenant-Colonel	D.J.R.	MBE RLC
Masterson	Lieutenant-Colonel	W.P.	Late RASC/RAOC
Maxwell	Lieutenant-Colonel	R.J.C.	MBE
McAllister	Lieutenant-Colonel	R.C.A.	Late RCT
McClellen	Captains	P. & S.	RLC
McCormack	Lieutenant-Colonel	H.D.	GM RLC
McCullough	Lieutenant-Colonel	L.M.	OBE, late RCT/ HAC/ WFR
McGill	Lieutenant	F.C.	RLC(V)
McHenry	Colonel	M.C.	US Army
McIntyre	Mr	N.	Late RCT
McPherson	Lieutenant-Colonel	I.A.	OBE BEM RLC
Messervy	Captain	S.M.	
Montgomerie	Major	H.M.	
Morley-Clarke	Mr	J.	BA (HONS)
Morris	Captain	P.D.	Late RAOC
Morton	Dr and Mrs	A.R.	
Morton	Mr and Mrs	D.	
Mosely	Second Lieutenant	J.C.	RLC
Murray	Major	J.	Late RCT
Nash	Corporal	A.J.	Late RASC
Neate	Major	B.C.	Late ACC
Neeves	Lieutenant-Colonel	B.C	
Newcombe	Colonel	J.A.	Late RCT
Nightingale	Brigadier	R.A.	MBE
Norman	Major	J.R.	TD RLC
Nunez	Corporal	F.A.A.	Late RASC
O'Leary	Lieutenant-Colonel	C.J.	RLC
O'Sullivan	Lieutenant-Colonel	G.A.	MBE QGM RLC
Owen	Lieutenant-Colonel	D.J.	MBE
Parkins	Warrant Officer 1	K.	RLC
Peacock	Lieutenant-Colonel	R.	RLC
Pearce	Lieutenant-Colonel	G.T.	MBE, late RCT
Pentland	Warrant Officer 1	D.C.	RLC
Perkins	Major	M.L.	TD
Pett	Captain	R.J.	
Phillips	Lieutenant-Colonel	A.W.	MBE RLC
Phillips	Major	R.C.	

Surname	Rank	Initials	Notes
Picot	Warrant Officer 1	I. K.	RLC
Plowright	Lieutenant-Colonel	N. R.	Late RCT/RLC
Powell	Captain	C. C.	Late RASC/RCT/RLC
Power	Mr	M.	Worshipful Company of Carmen
Pratt	Major	R. M.	RLC
Provan	Staff Sergeant	J.	RLC
Quist	Mr	B.	Late RASC
Randall	Mr	R. S.	
Ratazzi	Brigadier	R. E.	CBE, late RCT
Rathbone	Lieutenant	B.	Late RASC
Reason	Major	L. C. W.	Late RCT
Rees	Brigadier	I. D. O.	
Richards	Lieutenant-Colonel	M. J.	MBE RLC
Riggall	Colonel	J. S.	MBE, late RCT
Rintoul	Mr	G. F.	Late RAOC/RCT
Roberts	Lieutenant-Colonel	P. M. W.	Late RCT
Robertson	Lieutenant-Colonel	P. A.	RLC
Robertson	Captain	G. D.	RLC
Robinson	Captain	G. T. K.	Late RAOC
Robinson	Lieutenant-Colonel	P.	Late RASC/RCT
Ronald	Colonel	D. W.	Late RCT
Rook	Brigadier	R.	OBE
Roycroft	Brigadier and Mrs	M. J.	
Rust	Lieutenant-Colonel	M. J.	RLC
Sandberg	Brigadier	J. B.	CBE, late RASC
Saunders	Mr	R.	Royal Berkshire Regiment
Scott	Warrant Officer 1	W. N.	RLC
Seabury	Mr	F.	Late RASC
Shaw	Corporal	M. P.	
Shawley	Colonel	G. J.	TD
Small	Lieutenant-Colonel	R. S.	RLC
Smellie	Lieutenant-Colonel	N. A.	MBE RLC
Smetham	Lieutenant-Colonel	A. J. M.	Late RCT
Smith	Lieutenant-Colonel	R. C.	Late RCT
Smith	Captain	N. A.	Late RCT
Smith	Lieutenant	N. A.	RLC
St John	Major	C. J.	TD
Stanford	Captain	N. J.	RLC
Stanton	Colonel	W. E.	
Starling	Major	J. R.	RLC
Steirn	Brigadier	C.	Late RLC
Stone	Lieutenant-Colonel	R. J.	RE(TW)
Street	Sergeant	A. E.	Late RASC
Sutton	Brigadier	D. J.	OBE, late RCT
Swale	Major	M.	Late RCT
Symes	Brigadier	P. W.	Late RAOC
Tanswell	Major (OEO)	B.	Late RAOC
Tapp	Colonel	A. R.	Late RCT
Taylor	Lieutenant-Colonel	C. D.	Late RCT
Taylor	Warrant Officer 2	A.	Late P&CS
Thomas	Lieutenant-Colonel	R. E.	OBE, late RASC/RCT
Thorpe	Lieutenant-Colonel	P. J.	RLC
Tock	Major	B. J.	RLC
Tong	Major	J. E.	Late RCT
Tuhey	Captain	K.	TD RLC
Turner	Brigadier	J. A.	Late RAOC
Tutt	Colonel	K. M.	OBE ADC
Twitchett	Lieutenant-Colonel	H. R.	Late RASC/RCT
Vaughan	Mrs	B. C.	
Vickerman	Major	P. M.	RLC
Vickers	Major	M. D.	RLC
Waite-Roberts	Lieutenant-Colonel	E. J.	TD RLC (V)
Walke	Mr	S. J.	
Walke	Mrs	S. J.	
Walker	Colonel	J. S. M.	Late RCT
Wallace	Colonel	J. R.	OBE
Walton	Colonel	P. S.	Late RAOC
Watson	Colonel	A. G.	Late RCT
Webster	Warrant Officer 1 (Conductor)	G. C. V.	Late RAOC
Weekley	Lieutenant	I.	Late RASC
White	Major-General	M. S.	CB CBE DL
White	Mr	D. H.	Late RASC
Wilcox	Captain	J. J.	
Wilkinson	Lieutenant-Colonel	R. M.	
William	Staff Sergeant	M. B.	
Williams	Brigadier	G. D.	
Williams	Major	I.	
Williams	Major	P. N.	RLC
Winsor	Sergeant	R. C.	
Wiseman	Major	B.	
Woodward	Major	R. H.	TD
Worth	Private	I. S.	Late RAOC
Yeoman	Colonel	G. J.	MBE, late RCT
Young	Lieutenant-Colonel	M. H. G.	Late RCT
Young	Mr	A. J. G.	BEM, late RCT

INDEX